Theological Authority
in the Church

Theological Authority
in the Church

Reconsidering Traditionalism and Hierarchy

STEVEN NEMES

Foreword by Veli-Matti Kärkkäinen

CASCADE *Books* • Eugene, Oregon

THEOLOGICAL AUTHORITY IN THE CHURCH
Reconsidering Traditionalism and Hierarchy

Cascade Books
An Imprint of Wipf and Stock Publishers
199 W. 8th Ave., Suite 3
Eugene, OR 97401

www.wipfandstock.com

PAPERBACK ISBN: 978-1-6667-5258-8
HARDCOVER ISBN: 978-1-6667-5259-5
EBOOK ISBN: 978-1-6667-5260-1

Cataloguing-in-Publication data:

Names: Nemes, Steven, author. | Kärkkäinen, Veli-Matti, foreword.

Title: Theological authority in the church : reconsidering traditionalism and hierarchy / by Steven Nemes; foreword by Veli-Matti Kärkkäinen

Description: Eugene, OR: Cascade Books, 2023 | Includes bibliographical references and index.

Identifiers: ISBN 978-1-6667-5258-8 (paperback) | ISBN 978-1-6667-5259-5 (hardcover) | ISBN 978-1-6667-5260-1 (ebook)

Subjects: LCSH: Church. | Authority—Religious aspects—Christianity—History of doctrines. | Power (Christian theology)—History. | Christian leadership.

Classification: BV652.1 N46 2023 (paperback) | BV652.1 (ebook)

03/20/23

Nato caro uxorique amatae.
Cristian christianus sit.
Rachel ovis Dei sit.

"I am deaf to such words as, 'It is heretical, erroneous, an offense to pious ears.'"

"True piety demands, therefore, that one should hang upon the lips of the Lord and not hear or accept the word of any but the bridegroom."

"All those that teach in God's name should not sell their commands, ordinances, and burdens as God's, so that the yoke of his mercy should not become unpleasant to any one, but should leave them free."

"The whole of Christian life and salvation consists in this, that in Jesus Christ God has provided us with the remission of sins and everything else, and that we are to show forth and imitate Jesus Christ in our lives."

—HULDRYCH ZWINGLI

"Gentlemen, it is religion, the love of God and neighbour, which gives life a meaning; knowledge cannot do it."

—ADOLF VON HARNACK

"Religion that is pure and undefiled before God the Father is this: to care for orphans and widows in their distress and to keep oneself unstained by the world."

—JAMES 1:27

Contents

Foreword

MUCH HAS BEEN WRITTEN in church history and theology about the question of (ultimate) authority in the church. And much has been debated about the same issue. Just consider the many splits throughout history, not least during the times of the Reformation(s). Why then add yet another book on the topic? Haven't all arguments pro and con already been harnessed so many times, over and over again? Hasn't all the possible ingenuity and creativity of the best theological minds been tried in the court of ecclesial speculation?

Steven Nemes's innovative, bold, and counter-(ecclesio)cultural essay convinces us that no, not all has yet been said about this vital topic. Turning away from abstract speculations and metaphysical arguments—which, ironically, he would have been qualified to use very profitably, being, as he is, a professional philosopher and metaphysician!—Dr. Nemes rather goes straight to the New Testament accounts of the confrontations between the Matthean Jesus and the Pharisees in order to advance his thesis in support of what he calls a "low" conception of ecclesial authority in theology—"low" in the sense that the ultimate authority has not been given to any human tradition, nor to any group of people or even office, but rather only to Jesus and his teachings.

Gleaning also from other relevant parts of the New Testament and from the treasures of the leading fathers of the church, this essay makes a compelling argument against "traditionalism" and "hierarchism." Whereas "traditionalism" assigns authority to human-made allegedly binding rules and prescriptions, Jesus, in the author's interpretation, categorically rejects any such claim. Similarly, Nemes argues that no human conception of authority, whether episcopal or other, stands the test of Jesus's vehement rebuttal.

In light of his extensive biblical scrutiny, supported by early Christian witnesses, the book seeks to dismantle any programmatically traditionalist and hierarchical notion of the church. His main target is Roman

Catholicism, not only in her earlier historical incarnations but also in the aftermath of Vatican II. Canvassing the whole mass of arguments, the author makes an effort to rebut the justification of what he calls "high" model(s) of the authority of the church, in which either tradition or a group of people (or a particular office) usurps the ultimate authority.

Is the book's bold argument credible and compelling? In this estimation, the reader is helped by the many virtues the author brings to the task. First, as a philosopher-theologian he sets forth a tightly and rigorously developed claim, taking into thoughtful consideration various arguments. While impassioned, his writing is also clear, balanced, and straightforward. Second, relatedly, unlike many proponents of strong claims the author dares to take a careful look at the potential defeating arguments and considers their weight sympathetically and critically. This kind of self-critical consideration is another manifestation of Dr. Nemes's desire to invite other colleagues and interested persons into continuing dialogue and exchange of ideas. It is also evidence of theological maturity and competence.

Whether one agrees or disagrees with the book's argument concerning the "low" view of ecclesial authority in theology, scholars, ministers, and interested laypeople will greatly benefit from this study, not least as it concerns how to do rigorous theological study on a topic widely and deeply studied by former generations. Going back to the sources testifies to the living and dynamic nature of Christian tradition, rightly understood. Into that stream of ideas and convictions this study helps the reader tap.

The jury is still out on the question of the ultimate authority of the church. No one interested in the debate should miss this book's ingenious argument.

Veli-Matti Kärkkäinen

Preface

THIS IS A BOOK about theological authority. "Theological authority" is the authority to tell another person that something must (not) be done for the sake of entering into or preserving friendship with God. The point of the present work is to argue for a "low" conception of ecclesial authority in theology. Its principal contention is that, in this matter of theological authority, the words of God or of Jesus and the words of every mere human being must always be distinguished from one another. They are never "blended" into one; God and Jesus speak for themselves. The most theological authority in the church that mere human beings can have is that of fallibly and in principle reversibly testifying and bearing witness to what God or Jesus have said or done. But no mere human beings in the church have such authority as ever to be entitled to the unconditional obedience or submission of others. Friendship with God is thus neither a matter of a traditionalist deference to the opinions and preoccupations of past generations, nor of submission to ecclesial hierarchies.

These ideas explode both the religion of the Pharisees and the theological system of Roman Catholicism. It will be argued at some length that they are representative of how Jesus himself thought. This comes out especially in his polemics against the Pharisees as recorded in the Gospel according to Matthew. Faithfulness to the thought of Jesus in the matter of theological authority therefore means rejecting the Roman Catholic understanding as well. But it will also become evident that accepting these ideas of Jesus's requires a more radical rethinking of the exercise of theological authority in the church as a whole. They impose a reconsideration of the preoccupations of the church away from the speculative metaphysical questions with which theology in the catholic tradition was concerned for so many years toward more practical, experiential matters. These metaphysical speculations by which all the Christian confessions are distinguished from each other must be set to the side as debatable matters of opinion. The purpose of the present work is thus not only to answer a theoretical question about how theological authority is exercised in the context of the church as a whole but also to invite to a different conception about the value of theology and about what it means to be a Christian more generally. It is not only an argument against "traditionalist" and "hierarchical" conceptions of theological authority as expressed for example in Roman Catholic thought but also a critique of the concerns and preoccupations of Christians of a variety of confessional allegiances. There are better things to be doing, and Christians can easily be united around these better things once the obscure matters by which they are distinguished from each other and which have no clear basis in Jesus's actual teachings are relativized as matters of opinion about speculative questions and academic curiosities. Christian faith becomes principally ethical, spiritual, and practical in nature, rather than consisting in the contemplation and even dogmatic enforcement of metaphysical speculations.

The first part of the book spanning chapters 1–5 addresses the theoretical question of theological authority in the church according to teachings of Jesus and the actual recorded practice of the apostles in the New Testament. Its tone is more strictly academic. Chapters 6–7 respond to objections and deal with the consequences of this argument for what it means to be a Christian and the church or messianic community of Jesus. The tone there can at times be more impassioned and polemical, but everything said in the final two chapters must be read on the assumption that the case in the first part of the book has been proven.

At one point in my life, indeed for quite some time, I was seriously considering converting to Roman Catholicism, but I later decided firmly against it. This book is the partial concretization of my efforts to elucidate, both for myself and for others, some of the reasoning in favor of that decision as well as its ultimate consequences for Christian faith.

1

Introduction

STATEMENT OF THESIS

THE PRINCIPAL QUESTION WITH which the present essay is concerned is that of theological authority in the church. The "church" refers to the messianic community of believers in Jesus. "Theological authority" refers to the standing to tell other persons (not) to do or believe something for the sake of friendship with God. To exercise theological authority is thus to tell others that this or that thing must (not) be done if one is to enter into or remain in friendship with God. The matter to be investigated in the pages that follow is that of whether and how and by whom such authority is properly exercised in the context of the church. Who is it that can tell others (not) to do or believe this or that for the sake of being in God's good graces? Indeed, what is anyone's basis for doing this?

This book argues for a "low" conception of ecclesial authority in theology. Its central thesis is as follows:

> *God and Jesus alone exercise theological authority in an original, infallible, and in principle irreversible manner. All other persons exercise theological authority in a derivative manner by fallibly and in principle reversibly relating and bearing witness to the teachings of Jesus and the works of God in him.*

The teachings of Jesus and the works of God in him are thus the only "tools" by which all other persons in the church fallibly and reversibly exercise theological authority. The human word is only binding insofar as it succeeds in relating and bearing witness to the always distinct and separable divine word. These ideas can be further explained as follows.

CLARIFICATIONS AND DEFINITIONS

One can draw a distinction between the "original" and "derivative" possession of a quality. A thing possesses a quality "originally" if it possesses it simply in virtue of what it is. A thing possesses a quality "derivatively" if it possesses it only through the assistance of something else. This distinction can be made clear by means of various examples. Consider how a human being is originally capable of learning language but only derivatively possesses actual knowledge of the English language. The capacity to learn language belongs to human beings by nature. The actual knowledge of a particular language however only comes through the assistance of another. One is not born with knowledge of English but only with the potential to learn it. Or consider how the sun is originally luminous whereas the moon is only derivatively so. The moon is only luminous to the extent that it reflects the light being given to it by the sun, which itself possesses light in an original way. The moon has no light to give of its own. Or consider how fire is originally hot but a pot of beans held over the fire is only derivatively so. There is therefore a distinction between the "original" and "derivative" possession of a quality.

This distinction can be applied to the case of theological authority as follows. God and Jesus alone possess in an original way the right or standing to tell other persons (not) to do or believe something for the sake of friendship with God. This is to say that they possess this authority simply in virtue of themselves and not in virtue of anyone else. From this it follows that every other person possesses theological authority in the church only in a derivative way. They properly and legitimately exercise theological authority only by being assisted or enabled in some way by God or Jesus. This "derivative" exercise of theological authority consists in the attempt to bear witness and testify to others those things that have been taught with an original authority by God or Jesus himself: "Go therefore and make disciples of all nations, . . . teaching them to obey everything that I have commanded you" (Matt 28:19–20).[1] The teachings of Jesus and the works of God in him are thus the proper "tools" used to exercise theological authority in the church.

Every authority is an authority to do something or other. Consider how the police in society have the authority to make arrests and to enforce the law, or how a teacher has the authority to manage a classroom and to

---

1. All biblical translations are my own.

teach students about some subject matter, or how the quarterback on a football team has the authority to throw passes and to call plays for the rest of the offense. The exercise of authority likewise makes use of certain tools. The police enforce the law by means of their badges, cars, guns, and the like, just as a teacher manages a classroom through various techniques and the legitimation of his or her superiors, just as a quarterback exercises his authority by means of a playbook and the use of his body.

The fact that every authority is an authority to do something or other makes it possible to evaluate exercises of authority according to the categories of "legitimacy" and "success." An exercise of authority is "legitimate" or "illegitimate" depending on whether it is done by someone who really does have the standing to do what he or she has done. It can be legitimate in principle for the police to enter into a person's home and to arrest him or her if they should have the appropriate warrant and approval, but it is illegitimate for doctors or firefighters or ordinary citizens to do the same thing. Such is not their job. It is legitimate for a teacher to assign a paper or reward a detention to a student whose behavior is inappropriate, but it would be illegitimate for another student or a custodian to do so. It is legitimate for the quarterback to throw a pass from behind the line of scrimmage, but it is illegitimate for the wide receiver to throw a forward pass after having passed the line of scrimmage with the ball.

An exercise of authority is "successful" or "failed" depending on whether the purpose of that particular sort of authority has been achieved. The exercise of the authority to enforce the law is successful if the police end up arresting a person who is actually a criminal, but it is failed if they arrest someone innocent. A teacher succeeds in his or her enforcement of classroom discipline if the disciplined student was actually the one causing a disruption to the learning environment, but he or she fails if not. A quarterback succeeds in his task if a player on his own team catches his pass, but he fails in his task if the pass falls to the ground or else is caught by someone on the defense.

It is clearly possible for legitimacy and success as categories for the normative evaluation of exercises of authority to come apart. An exercise of authority may be legitimate but unsuccessful, or it may be illegitimate but successful, or it may also be both illegitimate and unsuccessful. The police may justly or unjustly arrest an innocent person or else unjustly arrest a guilty person. A teacher may fairly or unfairly punish a student who was actually disobedient or else wrongly punish an innocent student. The quarterback may complete an illegal pass or else throw an interception on a legal or illegal pass. The legitimacy and success of any exercise of authority are thus distinct from one another and not necessarily coincident.

Every exercise of authority is to be normatively evaluated with reference to its purpose or object. To say that an exercise of authority is "fallible" is to say that it may in principle have been illegitimate or unsuccessful. To say that an exercise of authority is "reversible" is to say that it may be corrected or else undone later in time by someone else.

The purpose of theological authority once more is to propose to others that something is or is not to be done or believed for the sake of friendship with God. This something is (not) to be done because it is (not) right, or it is (not) to be believed because it is (not) true. To say that God and Jesus alone exercise theological authority in an infallible and in principle irreversible manner is therefore to say that they alone cannot fail to meet the purpose of theological authority in their exercises of it. Everything that they propose (not) be done or believed for the sake of friendship with God is actually (not) right or true and a genuine condition of such friendship. God and Jesus are not legitimately called into question nor corrected by anyone else on any matter; they alone are "unconditional" authorities. To say that the exercise of theological authority on the part of anyone else is fallible and reversible in principle is to say that every other person's exercise of theological authority may have been either illegitimate or unsuccessful. It is illegitimate if the person does not actually have the standing to propose that something in particular be done or believed for the sake of friendship with God, and it is unsuccessful if what the person proposes be done or believed is not actually right or true or a condition of friendship with God. Appeals to personal authority would therefore be illegitimate, while appeals to things not taught or demanded by God or Jesus would be unsuccessful. And to say that every other person's exercise of theological authority is reversible in principle is to say that every other person can in principle be called into question and corrected by someone else within the messianic community of God and Jesus.

RESTATEMENT OF THE THESIS

These definitions and clarifications make it possible to restate the thesis and vision of the present essay in a more precise and detailed form. The idea is that God and Jesus alone exercise theological authority in an original, infallible, and in principle irreversible way. This is to say that they alone can propose that other persons (not) do or believe things for the sake of friendship with God in such a way that they cannot in principle be called into question or corrected by others with respect to the legitimacy or success of their proposals. Every other person in the church exercises theological authority in a derivative, fallible, and in principle reversible manner. The

teachings of Jesus and works of God in him are the "tools" by which this authority is exercised, and its exercise by everyone else in the church is fallible
and in principle reversible. This is to say that no one else in the church has
any further theological authority than that of relating and bearing witness
to the teachings of Jesus and the works of God in him and applying them in
some particular context in such a way as always to be open to the correction
or critique of others in principle.

The present essay will attempt to substantiate this thesis through the
interpretation of the New Testament. It will offer interpretations of key passages from the Gospels, Acts, and Epistles. It will not address in very much
detail other strictly theological, philosophical, or historical questions that
are also relevant to this problem of theological authority. These issues have
already been discussed at some length in other works.[2] The purpose of the
present work is simply to show that the philosophical-theological vision
that was advocated for in these other places is not foreign to the thinking
of the earliest generation of the church as recorded in the New Testament.
Neither will the present work be concerned with taking a definite stance on
various matters of theological controversy. The goal is not to advocate for
this or that contested theological opinion but only to address the question of
what the New Testament teaches about theological authority in the church.

One might wonder: Why bother asking this question at all? Of course,
in itself it is a theologically interesting question, but it also has far-reaching
practical consequences. The truth is that there has been in recent times a
veritable "exodus" of persons from various forms of evangelical and Protestant Christianity into Roman Catholicism. Scot McKnight already noted
this phenomenon in an article published twenty years ago.[3] It seems that this
trend has not abated since then but may have even grown. Perhaps the most
famous such recent example is Scott Hahn.[4] Alongside him are a number
of academic philosophers, theologians, and ministers.[5] Notably, one of the
principal motivations commonly raised by those who make such an ecclesial conversion is precisely this issue of theological authority in the church.
In one recent volume, the philosophers Edward Feser, J. Budziszewski, Neal
Judisch, and Logan Paul Gage share this concern as a factor that prompted
their own conversions.[6] Similar stories are also found in the testimonies of
Douglas Beaumont, Brandon Dahm, and other former students of Southern

2. See Nemes, *Orthodoxy and Heresy*; Nemes, *Theology of the Manifest*.
3. McKnight, "From Wheaton to Rome," 451–72.
4. See Hahn and Hahn, *Rome Sweet Home*.
5. Besong and Fuqua, *Faith and Reason*.
6. See Besong and Fuqua, *Faith and Reason*, 20–23 and their respective chapters.

Evangelical Seminary.[7] These persons express a serious concern about the lack of a centralized authority in Protestantism for deciding matters of theological disagreement. Roman Catholicism purportedly offers them what they think is missing in the Protestant circles from which they left. McKnight thus writes in this respect that it is typical for converts to Roman Catholicism to want "to transcend the human limits of interpretive diversity to find an interpretive authority."[8]

The opinion of the present author is that such concerns for a living, centralized theological authority as motivate conversion to Roman Catholicism are in fact alien to the teachings of Jesus and his closest disciples. Jesus himself did not leave in the church what these persons are looking for; indeed, what Jesus actually teaches fatally undermines the very supposition of such a thing in the church in the first place, since his conception of how theological authority should function in the church is a quite different one. This means that these persons' desire for a living, centralized authority that can in principle resolve any theological dispute and impose a unity of opinion is fictive and has no basis in what Jesus actually taught; theological authority in the church does not function in the way that Roman Catholicism imagines. The goal of the present work is thus to substantiate this opinion by means of the interpretation of the New Testament. But it will also become evident in time that the line of argument pursued below will prove radically consequential for Christian theology as a whole. Indeed, it will require a rethinking of the nature of Christian faith and the unity of the church as well as of the priorities of Christian theology for the future, away from matters of dogma and speculative metaphysics to matters of ethics, spirituality, and practice. Christian life must be understood differently.

The perspective being proposed in the pages below is thus intended as an alternative to the "high" conception of ecclesial authority in theology that was quite popular and significant in the history of the church. This "high" conception is committed to two ideas about the way theological authority in the church functions. They are here going to be called "traditionalism" and "hierarchy." These points can be understood as follows.

7. Beaumont, *Evangelical Exodus.*
8. McKnight, "From Wheaton to Rome," 460.

2

"Traditionalism" and "Hierarchy"

INITIAL DEFINITIONS

"Traditionalism" as the term is used here refers to the idea that a particular community in one generation can come to make definitive and binding decisions about what it will practice or believe from that moment on into the future. These decisions are "definitive" in the sense that they are intended never to be revised or corrected after the fact, and they are "binding" in the sense that the consequence for the willful rejection of them is exclusion from the community. The definitive and binding nature of these decisions thus imposes a kind of retrospective or "traditionalist" loyalty to the past as a condition of group membership going forward. Membership in the group becomes a matter of belonging to a well-defined preexisting tradition. A group can therefore be called "traditionalist" if it understands itself in more or less these terms.

"Hierarchy" as the term is used here refers to the idea that a particular community is intrinsically structured in such a way that certain persons within it have the right and standing (at least on occasion) to demand things of others without opening themselves up to correction or legitimate refusal. They do not (at least in certain circumstances) have to win over the obedience of others through convincing argumentation or a demonstration of the propriety of what they propose. It is enough (at least on occasion) that they have said a thing and it must be obeyed insofar as they possess a certain rank

1

within the hierarchy of the community as a whole. A group can therefore be called "hierarchical" if it understands itself in more or less these terms.

"Traditionalism" and "hierarchy" are very closely related and even mutually reinforcing ideas. The definitive and binding quality of the decisions reached by some in the community is often taken to be grounded in the fact that it is the unique prerogative of certain members of the hierarchy to make such decisions on behalf of the group as a whole. They are definitive and binding on everyone within the group precisely because they are decisions made by persons of a certain appropriate rank or office. A "traditionalist" group is thus likely to be "hierarchical" as well. These ideas can therefore be understood as two dimensions of a "high" view of ecclesial authority in theology. On the other hand, the rejection of either idea affects the interpretation of the other. Rejecting "traditionalism" means that no particular generation of a group is necessarily beholden to the practices and opinions of an earlier one. No past generation of a group can definitively bind future generations of the same group to its own opinions and practices. The rejection of "traditionalism" thus can also undermine the pretense to authority implied in "hierarchy." The authorities of past generations are checked by those of future generations. Rejecting "hierarchy" on the other hand means making the "traditionalism" of a group to function by means of consensus. No one possesses such a rank as to be entitled to the unconditional obedience of all others in any circumstance, so that no decision can be binding upon everyone else without the free consent of the whole group. Only thus can the opinions of one generation be passed on to later ones.

This is how "traditionalism" and "hierarchy" are mutually reinforcing ideas that together serve the purpose of making it possible for a community to establish, preserve, and even further specify its unity and identity over time in a maximally efficient way. A community can be called both "traditionalist" and "hierarchical" to the extent that it functions according to these ideas. "Traditionalism" makes it possible for a group to draw clear boundaries regarding its practice and belief on pain of exclusion. "Hierarchy" makes it possible for these drawn boundaries to be justified by appeal to the institutional authority of the persons who draw them on behalf of the group. The denial of either or both ideas would inevitably lead to a radically different self-conception of the identity of a group. And it can also be seen that they are not unfamiliar ideas in the history of theology.

THE PHARISEES AND ROMAN CATHOLICISM

"Traditionalism" and "hierarchy" appear to have been operative ideas in the theological self-understanding of Pharisees. This is how one can say that they possessed a "high" view of "ecclesial" or community authority in matters of theology.

Just who were the Pharisees? Hyam Maccoby writes that they were the progenitors of what later would become rabbinic Judaism.[1] Yet the precise details of this opinion are strongly contested by more recent writers. Günter Stemberger, for example, wishes to distinguish the historical Pharisees from later generations of rabbis who appropriated them (whether rightly or wrongly) as spiritual ancestors.[2] The controversy has to do with the extent to which the *pharisaioi* of the Greek sources (such as Josephus and the New Testament) overlap with the *perushim* of later rabbinic ones. The words are not always used clearly as synonyms, neither do the rabbis always use the term *perushim* to refer to groups with which they identify. John Bowker thus writes that "the sense in which the Pharisees were the predecessors of the rabbis is by no means simple or direct. Nothing could be more misleading than to refer to the Pharisees without further qualification as the predecessors of the rabbis, for the fact remains that 'Pharisees' are attacked in rabbinic sources as vigorously as 'Pharisees' are attacked in the Gospels, and often for similar reasons."[3] Bowker thinks it is sooner more plausible to connect the "Pharisees" and the rabbis with the Hakamim or "Sages."[4] These persons arose within Israel with a concern to motivate ritual purity and holiness for all Jews through the interpretation of the Law for their present day.[5] There is admittedly no space here to discuss this matter in any detail, but what matters for present purposes are certain facts over which there is no controversy at all.

These Hakamim were convinced that obedience to Torah is not merely a matter of interpreting it for the present day but also of recognizing that "Torah had already been applied and 'lived out' by earlier figures."[6] From this conviction came the conclusion that "the long tradition of what it has meant in practice to obey Torah (and equally to disobey Torah) is in a sense

1. Maccoby, *Early Rabbinic Writings*, 9–16.
2. Stemberger, "Pharisees and the Rabbis."
3. Bowker, *Jesus and the Pharisees*, 1.
4. Bowker, *Jesus and the Pharisees*, 6.
5. Bowker, *Jesus and the Pharisees*, 17.
6. Bowker, *Jesus and the Pharisees*, 17.

as important as Torah itself."[7] And so the Pharisees are likewise said by Josephus to have accepted an "oral Torah" or more precisely oral traditions of their ancestors in addition to the written Torah of the books of Moses.[8] Menahem Mansoor says of the Pharisees that they "admitted the validity of an evolutionary and non-literal approach toward the legal decisions and regarded the legal framework of the Oral Law as equally valid as the Written Law."[9] This oral law is defined by Maccoby as "a living, growing body of law and lore, responding to changing circumstances and becoming more comprehensive in scope as the unfolding of time posed new questions."[10] The principal theological conviction of the Pharisees was thus that God's commandments "were to be interpreted in conformity with the standard and interpretation of the rabbis of each generation, and to be made to harmonize with advanced ideas."[11] And Bowker writes further: "It is clear from Josephus that a fundamental and differentiating characteristic [of the Pharisees] was their adherence to the Law together with a procedure of traditional interpretation which established a relation between the Law as originally given and the customary application of it by the people."[12] Each generation of teachers—although not necessarily others within the community—had the authority to "bind" and to "loose." And Josephus even speaks of the Pharisees as binding and loosing "at their pleasure."[13] This was the authority to permit or oblige or forbid certain ideas or practices as well as the right to include or exclude certain persons from the community.[14]

One can therefore see that the Pharisees were both "traditionalist" and "hierarchical." "Traditionalism" was at work because they took the rabbis and teachers of each generation to be capable of making decisions that were definitive and binding for later generations. Those in the future would have to accept and submit to the various decisions of those from the past. Being a member of this group in the present was always a matter of sharing the commitments and preoccupations of past members. This is an illustration of the idea that the interpretation of the Law had to be consonant with the definitive and binding determinations of past sages and rabbis.[15] The deci-

---

7. Bowker, *Jesus and the Pharisees*, 17–18.

8. Josephus, *Ant.* 13:297.

9. Mansoor, "Pharisees," 30.

10. Maccoby, *Early Rabbinic Writings*, 4.

11. Mansoor, "Pharisees," 31.

12. Bowker, *Jesus and the Pharisees*, 2.

13. Josephus, *War* 1:111.

14. Singer, *Jewish Encyclopedia*, 215; cf. Mansoor, "Pharisees," 31.

15. Berger, *Rabbinic Authority*, 65.

sions of one generation of rabbis thus imposed limits upon what can be said by later generations. And "hierarchy" was at work because not just anyone could make these decisions but only authorized teachers. One needed to be "ordained" by someone else who already possessed the appropriate authority himself.[16] These decisions were binding and definitive precisely because they were made by the right persons with the right rank. An example of this system is found in the famous story of the "excommunication" of rabbi Eliezer ben Hurcanus as retold in b. Bava Metzia 59b.[17] The rabbis were debating whether an earthenware vessel cut widthwise into segments and extended by placing sand between the segments is ritually pure or impure. Rabbi Eliezer had an opinion that all the other rabbis rejected. He was able to respond to every objection and even to conjure miracles in defense of his opinion. Yet his interpretation was rejected, and he was excluded from the community by a majority rule.

Roman Catholicism also has a "traditionalist" and "hierarchical" understanding of the church. These are dimensions of its "high" view of ecclesial authority in theology. This emerges especially clearly from the formal statement of its conception of the episcopate as explained in the "Dogmatic Constitution on the Church" (*Lumen Gentium*) of 1964 and "Dogmatic Constitution on Divine Revelation" (*Dei Verbum*) of 1965 promulgated at the Second Vatican Council. In these documents the bishops are understood to be the successors of the apostles as the chief shepherds of Jesus's church in his physical absence. They "preside in the place of God" over the flock.[18] They alone possess the right to the "authentic" or authoritative interpretation of the word of God for the whole community.[19] Persons are welcomed into this class through the sacrament of holy orders by means of the rite of consecration: "It pertains to the bishops to admit newly elected members into the Episcopal body by means of the sacrament of Orders."[20] The episcopate thus forms a kind of "closed circle." One can only enter the circle by being welcomed by another already found in it. And by this sacramental consecration the bishops thereby receive a special charism or gift/grace of the Holy Spirit. It is in virtue of this charism that they "in an

---

16. Berger, *Rabbinic Authority*, chs. 3–4.

17. Maccoby, *Early Rabbinic Writings*, 5. The story from the Babylonian Talmud can be read online for free at https://www.sefaria.org/Bava_Metzia.59b.

18. Paul VI, *Lumen Gentium* (*LG* hereafter) 20.

19. Paul VI, *Dei Verbum* (*DV* hereafter) 10.

20. *LG* 21.

eminent and visible way sustain the roles of Christ himself as Teacher, Shepherd and High Priest, and . . . act in his person."[21]

Roman Catholicism further teaches that this special charism associated with the episcopate makes it possible for the bishops to act infallibly on certain occasions. The modern statement of this idea comes in *Lumen Gentium*. The bishops are said to teach infallibly when all of them scattered throughout the world and in communion with each other happen to agree upon some matter as essential to the faith. They also teach infallibly when gathered in an ecumenical council for the sake of defining some matter of the faith. And the bishop of Rome in particular can teach infallibly when proposing statements and definitions on matters of faith and morals entirely on his own if he should see fit to do so. His proclamations are "of themselves, and not from the consent of the Church, . . . justly styled irreformable, since they are pronounced with the assistance of the Holy Spirit, promised to him in blessed Peter, and therefore they need no approval of others, nor do they allow an appeal to any other judgment."[22] These are therefore the conditions in which the exercise of theological authority on the part of the magisterium of the church is said to be infallible.

One can thus see both "traditionalism" and "hierarchy" at work in Roman Catholicism as well. This conception of the church is "traditionalist" because it asserts that the church has the right to make definitive and binding statements in matters of practice and belief on pain of exclusion from the community. Any person from within the community who does not submit to the authoritative pronouncements of the church falls under the weight of an anathema and excommunication. There is, for example, no such thing as a properly faithful Roman Catholic who consciously rejects Chalcedonian Christology or the perpetual virginity of Mary. This reality imposes a retrospective or "traditionalist" deference to the ideas of certain important past figures on the part of anyone who would be a part of this communion. It is likewise "hierarchical" because these decisions are not the prerogative of anyone other than the bishops of the church. Only those persons who possess the title of bishop within its hierarchy can claim this right, and on certain occasions they cannot be legitimately called into question or contradicted. The *ex cathedra* definitions of the Pope, for example, "of themselves, and not from the consent of the Church, . . . need no approval of others, nor do they allow an appeal to any other judgment."

There is of course the following noteworthy difference between the religion of the Pharisees and Roman Catholicism. Roman Catholicism

21. *LG* 21.
22. *LG* 25.

understands infallibility as divine protection from error in teaching, as Hans Küng defines it: "Infallibility is defined as the impossibility of falling into error."[23] God providentially protects the church's magisterium from making erroneous pronouncements in the appropriate conditions. It likewise teaches that the task of the magisterium of the church is not that of inventing doctrine but rather of serving the superior word of God by its authoritative interpretation, as in *Dei Verbum*: "teaching only what has been handed on, listening to it devoutly, guarding it scrupulously and explaining it faithfully in accord with a divine commission and with the help of the Holy Spirit."[24] On the other hand, Maccoby notes that there is nothing in rabbinic Jewish self-understanding that corresponds to the Roman Catholic notion of the "infallibility" of the church.[25] There is the whole tractate m. Horayot dedicated to the question of how to address errors of various sorts by the Council.[26] Michael Berger likewise argues that the understanding of "infallibility" in rabbinic thinking is very controverted and difficult. It depends on whether one understands the rabbis to be involved in the retrospective passing-on of a well-defined original oral Torah or else in a forward-looking and constructive project of developing an inchoate first deposit.[27] The latter perspective is the more popular one, and it does not make for rabbinic "infallibility" in the sense of protection from error but rather rabbinic "finality." It is not that the rabbis cannot be mistaken but that their legitimately reached decisions are final and irreversible insofar as there is no greater court of appeal beyond them. These differences are consequently worth keeping in mind.

THEOLOGICAL CONSEQUENCES

Accepting "traditionalism" in conjunction with "hierarchy" is theologically significant. Both the Pharisees and Roman Catholicism would admit that the exercise of theological authority by their respective hierarchies is strictly derivative in nature. The authority of any particular generation of teachers is derivative upon their inclusion into a special class of interpreters through ordination by those who came before them. The authority of any particular bishops is derivative upon their succession to the position of authority that Jesus himself granted to the apostles. And both the Pharisees and Roman

23. Küng, *Infallible?*, 55.

24. *DV* 10.

25. Maccoby, *Early Rabbinic Writings*, 4–5.

26. This can be read online at https://www.sefaria.org/Mishnah_Horayot.

27. Berger, *Rabbinic Authority*, 64–67.

Catholicism would accept that the elders, apostles, and bishops only exercise authority in the community of God's people because this privilege was ultimately given to them by God himself. Yet both also maintain that it is possible for an exercise of theological authority to be strictly derivative and yet functionally original. To call it "strictly derivative" is to say that it is not exercised solely by God or Jesus himself but rather by some other person or group necessarily enabled by them in some way. It is not a word coming straight from the mouth of God or Jesus; it is rather spoken by someone who is authorized and in some way enabled to speak with authority by God or Jesus. But to call it "functionally original" is to say that it is to be treated and received in the community as having the same significance and importance as though God or Jesus were the one speaking. It is "infallible" and in principle irreversible despite being derivative. This is therefore the consequence of combining "traditionalism" and "hierarchy" in the theological context: the word of mere human beings—a tradition of the elders; a sentence propagated by an ecumenical council or defined *ex cathedra* by the bishop of Rome; etc.—can rightly be used as a "tool" for exercising theological authority with the same effect as if it were a word right out of the mouth of God or Jesus himself.

One may explain this functional originality in a variety of ways. One can say with the Pharisees that there is no greater court of appeal than the relevant authorities. The elders exercise functionally original authority because God has granted them alone the final say about these matters; there is no one else established by God with the standing to contradict or question them.[28] This point was mentioned earlier. Or one may say, with Thomas Joseph White, that in Roman Catholicism God himself providentially arranges things in such a way that definitive and binding magisterial statements made in certain conditions are guaranteed by him not to be in error.[29] One might even propose that there is a kind of "dual agency" taking place in these situations: God is making use of the church or of its magisterium in its historical development as an instrument for exercising his own original theological authority.[30] It is not "only" the church speaking but rather God speaking through the church over time; the church becomes a mouthpiece for God's expression of his will and truth in a way that does not apply to everything else under his providential control. "Dual agency" thus means infallibility by means of providential guidance, and this "dual agency" is reliably discerned where the stipulated conditions of infallibility obtain. God

28. Berger, *Rabbinic Authority*, 64.

29. White, *Light of Christ*, 182–84.

30. White, *Light of Christ*, 186.

speaks through history and his voice is particularly clearly heard where the magisterium of the church makes its pronouncements. It is in a sense a matter of both God and human beings speaking the same thing whenever those conditions are found.

There are consequently different possibilities for understanding how a strictly derivative exercise of theological authority can also be functionally original. The Pharisees think in terms of "finality," while Roman Catholicism prefers instead a notion of "dual agency." But where the two systems are agreed is in the idea that such strictly derivative but functionally original exercises of theological authority are in fact possible. They both affirm a "high" view of ecclesial or community authority in matters of theology. Something that was spoken by otherwise mere human beings can have the same weight and authority as though it had come from the mouth of God himself—this is the ultimate and most significant consequence of combining "traditionalism" with "hierarchy."

The perspective offered in the present work is adamantly opposed to this scheme. It proposes a "low" view of ecclesial authority in theology. It maintains that God and Jesus alone exercise theological authority in the church in an original, infallible, and in principle irreversible way; every other person's exercise of theological authority is only ever derivative, fallible, and reversible in principle. God's and Jesus's exercise of theological authority is infallible and in principle irreversible precisely because it is original; everyone else's exercise of theological authority is fallible and reversible in principle precisely because it is derivative. Only the word that comes straight from the mouth of God or of Jesus is unconditionally authoritative in theology; the human word is only ever conditionally and contingently authoritative. This of course implies that there is a higher court of appeal than any particular person or group of persons within the messianic community of the church. This court of appeal consists of the teachings of God the Father and Jesus his Son. Anything that any other person says in the church can and should always be judged according to this higher court of appeal. Nothing is obligatory which it does not oblige, nor anything permitted which it forbids. The appeal to it is always fallible and so reversible in principle, so that the pretense to "finality" is thus unfounded. But the present thesis also implies that the divine word is always distinct and separable from the human word. Only thus can the comparison between the one and the other be made. This means that the one is only ever fallible in relation to the other. There is no guarantee of providential protection from error pertaining to the teaching authorities of the church—except insofar as a person manages successfully to relate and bear witness to what Jesus Christ himself has taught apart from him or her. There is no such thing as "dual agency" in the matter of magisterial pronouncements, because there is always a certain "distance" of agency between God and Jesus and every mere human speaker. And this means that it is always possible for a person within the church other than Jesus or God to have erred in his or her understanding of things. These are therefore the fundamental points of difference between the perspectives.

PREVIEW OF THE ARGUMENT

The argumentation of the present work will be as follows. It is taken for granted that God and Jesus exercise theological authority in an original way. This implies that their exercises of authority are also infallible and in principle irreversible. But the conjunction of "traditionalism" and "hierarchy" in the understanding of the church entails that persons other than God or Jesus can exercise theological authority in a strictly derivative but functionally original way. The case will be made that Jesus rejects this idea altogether. He more specifically rejects both "traditionalism" and "hierarchy" as a part of his regular polemic against the Pharisees. It is not just that particular ideas constituting the content of Pharisaic religion are rejected, but rather that the very structure of Pharisaical religion itself as intrinsically "traditionalist" and "hierarchical" is rejected. From this it follows that these ideas must be rejected as applying to the church or messianic community of Jesus as well. His polemics against the Pharisees subsequently serve as an argument against interpreting him along "traditionalist" and "hierarchical" lines as in Roman Catholicism. Jesus's rejection of "traditionalism" and "hierarchy" in the Pharisees also motivates the rejection of Roman Catholicism which functions by these same ideas.

3

Against "Traditionalism"

"TRADITIONALISM" IS THE IDEA that one generation of a group can make a decision about some matter of practice or belief that is definitive and binding for all future generations on pain of exclusion from the community itself. This implies that membership in the group functions by means of a "traditionalist" deference to the preoccupations and ideas of past generations. It is one dimension of a "high" view of ecclesial or community authority in theology. This idea was operative in the religious understanding of the Pharisees. John Bowker writes that "the Pharisaioi/Ḥakamim took the side of the people in defending the validity of custom and tradition as a legitimate means of understanding (and implementing) the intentions of Torah."[1] This "traditionalism" of the Pharisees is principally addressed in the incident regarding the washing of hands in conformity with the "traditions of the elders" (Matt 15:1–9/Mark 7:1–13).

THE TRADITIONS OF THE ELDERS

The Pharisees object to the fact that Jesus's disciples do not follow these traditions by washing their hands before eating. Presumably Jesus did not do this either.[2] Luke 11:37–38 reports that Jesus did not ritually wash his hands before eating. This tradition of the elders apparently did not matter to him. Jesus therefore responds to the Pharisees' objection by claiming that their traditions lead them to break God's commandments. God specifically

1. Bowker, *Jesus and the Pharisees*, 30.
2. Turner, *Matthew*, 378.

had commanded children to honor their parents and not curse them, and yet the Pharisees permit that a person consecrate to God whatever funds might normally have gone toward the care of his parents. They allow that a person not take care of his parents by consecrating his money to God.[3] This for Jesus amounts to a breaking of the commandments. Craig Blomberg thus writes of the Pharisees: "The temple worship and its ritual are scrupulously supported but at the expense of a genuine relationship with the living God that recognizes the priorities of human need and does not erect institutions and rules that inhibit social and interpersonal responsibility."[4] Jesus then concludes that Isaiah was right to prophesy about them: "This people honors me with their lips, but their hearts are far from me; in vain do they worship me, teaching human precepts as doctrines" (Matt 15:8–9; cf. Isa. 29:13). He summarizes the point: "You abandon the commandment of God and hold to human tradition" (Mark 7:9).

Exactly how does this constitute an argument against "traditionalism"? Anthony Saldarini summarizes the point well: "In this passage the Pharisees and scribes defend the tradition of the elders . . . and Jesus defends the more important commandments of God."[5] There are two things to note. First, Jesus utterly disregards the Pharisees' appeal to the traditions of the elders. He feels no need to follow these traditions which admittedly have no basis in a publicly attested divine commandment.[6] Second, Jesus then raises an argument against the Pharisees' concern about these traditions in general. He claims that the Pharisees do wrong in preferring merely human traditions to the word of God. It is implied that they should always rather compare and subordinate human words to the divine word. But this presupposes that the human word and divine word are always distinct and separately given. This is therefore the substance of his rejection of their "traditionalism." Human words are not binding except as bearing witness to the independent divine word. Human words must always be compared and subordinated to the publicly attested divine word and never confused with it. There is no strictly derivative but functionally original exercise of theological authority.

Yet it must be noted that Jesus's polemics can seem highly unnuanced and simplistic from the point of view of a "traditionalist" theology. He says that the Pharisees prefer their traditions to the commandment of God. A number of possible responses from the "traditionalist" side immediately suggest themselves, some of which will be enumerated below. Suppose then

3. Turner, *Matthew*, 380; Carson, "Matthew," 348.

4. Blomberg, *Matthew*, 239.

5. Saldarini, *Pharisees, Scribes and Sadducees*, 166.

6. Turner, *Matthew*, 378–79.

that one assumes Jesus to be a "traditionalist." This passage can give the impression that Jesus does not know how to argue well from within his own paradigm of thought. But this apparent simplicity could be deceptive. It may be that Jesus's argument is so simple precisely because he does not accept the legitimacy of the possible lines of response that the Pharisees might have offered on behalf of their "traditionalism." Perhaps he rejects the essential ideas of the "traditionalist" paradigm altogether.

The argument will therefore be as follows. Jesus neither acts nor argues like a "traditionalist." He disregards a tradition with some weight behind it, and he argues that the Pharisees do wrong in preferring human traditions to the divine commandments. His objection to the Pharisees would admittedly be very weak if he accepted the theoretical framework of the "traditionalist" paradigm, but it would be strong indeed if he rejected the "traditionalist" idea that human words can on whatever basis be used as "tools" for exercising theological authority. And presumably Jesus thought his own argument was a strong one. This therefore suggests that Jesus rejected "traditionalism." These points can be explained in some detail as follows.

Jesus seems clearly to be operating from outside of the "traditionalist" paradigm altogether. He does not act or reason like someone who believes that past figures have "authority to teach doctrine," as J. Budziszewski says about the Roman Catholic Church.[7] The fact that certain unnamed "elders" have passed down some traditional practice of ritual handwashing before eating means nothing to him. Neither he nor his disciples follow it. They presumably feel no necessity in observing it because there is no divine commandment to do so. David Turner thus writes that Jesus "does not view these traditions as having authority on a par with the written Torah."[8] But consider too the way in which Jesus objects to the Pharisees. It does not matter to him for example that the Pharisees might have proposed a differentiation of teachings with varied levels of authority. He does not consider that the washing of hands might bear more weight for them as a tradition than the teaching about consecrating money to God. Neither does it matter to him what narrative the Pharisees might have offered in defense of their authority to interpret the Law and make such allowances for people. He does not make any reference to the illegitimacy of their ordination or anything of the sort. He certainly does not consider that God himself has given a kind of sovereign and free interpretative authority to the elders to "bind" and "loose" as they please. Neither does he believe that God might be understood providentially to be using the elders as an instrument for

7. Budziszewski, "Rake's Progress," 74.
8. Turner, *Matthew*, 380.

the proclamation of the truth. None of this comes up at all. He simply and plainly says that they prefer human traditions to the word of God (Matt 15:6/Mark 7:8–9).

What does it mean that the Pharisees prefer human traditions to the word of God? The presuppositions of this claim in the light of the way it functions within Jesus's argument should be elucidated. It is not necessarily that the Pharisees themselves explicitly admit or confess that human tradition is more important than the word of God. This incidentally does seem to have been the opinion of the rabbis who excommunicated Eliezer ben Hurcanus at b. Bava Metzia 59b. They believed that the task of the interpretation of Torah was left to human beings alone and specifically the rabbis. They (wrongly) appealed to Exod 23:2 to justify their right: "Follow a majority." This is a wrong appeal because the text actually says: "You shall not follow a majority in wrongdoing; when you bear witness in a lawsuit, you shall not side with the majority so as to pervert justice." But the rabbis are convinced that the decision must be made by majority rule. They further believe that they alone have the authority to make pronouncements in the interpretation of the Law. This means that the divine signs and miracles and even the voice from heaven do not count in favor of Eliezer's opinion as long as the majority of rabbis disagree with it. As Hyam Maccoby writes: "God, having given the rabbis the right of decision by majority vote, could not intervene to influence the discussions of the rabbis!"[9] The text thus relates how God reacted to the excommunication of Eliezer: "My children have triumphed over me."[10] They triumphed over God because they allowed nothing other than their own judgments and authority to determine what was to be done in an interpretive dispute. This may or may not have been the perspective of the Pharisees with which Jesus was interacting here. But the significance of his argument against them is the same in either case. The problem with them is that they put human tradition functionally on a par with the word of God. They are willing in principle to grant to human tradition the same finality and irreversibility one would grant to the word of God, and this also means that they will end up preferring human tradition to the word of God when the two come into contradiction. How so?

It is apparently not a part of the Pharisees' method to hold the officially sanctioned human word in subordination to the divine word. They rather try to see the divine word through the lens of the officially sanctioned human word. They try to understand what God says through the lens of what others have said. But this means that they will not be properly disposed to

9. Maccoby, *Early Rabbinic Writings*, 5.
10. Maccoby, *Early Rabbinic Writings*, 5.

see the contradictions when they arise because they are always starting from the assumption of two ultimate sources instead of just one. They will not be properly aware of it when one source comes to disagree with the other but will rather be predisposed to read the divine word in such a way that it only ever agrees with the human word. The divine word will inevitably be adjusted to the human word. This is part and parcel of the attitude of retrospective deference motivated by their "traditionalism."

Jesus's opinion is contrary to this. His argument assumes that every human word, irrespective of its "official" or "traditional" status, must be subordinated to the divine word. D. A. Carson thus comments: "[Jesus] made a fundamental distinction between 'the command of God' (as found in Scripture) and the Halakhic tradition."[11] For Jesus, a teaching need not be accepted just because it is passed down as a part of some tradition. This alone would not make it binding on anyone. It must rather be judged according to God's teachings. The teachings of God that come from his mouth are alone the proper "tools" for exercising theological authority. These divine words alone can determine unconditionally what a person is or is not to do for the sake of entering into or preserving friendship with God, and the merely human word can be ignored, or even rejected if it implies disobedience to one of God's commands. But this proposed subordination and comparison also assumes that every human word is always distinct and separable from the divine word. Only thus can the one be subordinated to and measured against the other. This means further that the official sanction of certain developments of tradition within the community of God's people is not necessarily indicative of God's approval. God and human beings always act freely of one another in the sense that what is approved by one is not necessarily approved by the other. And from all these assumptions—the subordination of the human word to the divine, as well as their fundamental distinction and separation—it will clearly follow that Jesus rejects not only the particular traditions of the Pharisees but even their "traditionalism" as such. As Carson writes: "The judgment is so sweeping that it calls into question not only the Jews' Halakah but their entire worship and teaching."[12] This can be explained as follows.

The implicit assumption of Jesus's argument is that every tradition and teaching of human beings must be measured against the standard of the commandment of God. Otherwise it would not be objectionable for the Pharisees to prefer human traditions to the commandment of God. They could claim that they have done nothing wrong because not every tradition

11. Carson, "Matthew," 348.
12. Carson, "Matthew," 349.

and teaching of human beings needs to be measured against the standard of the commandment of God. They could claim that the teaching of the elders has a certain "finality" to it independently of its basis in the written Torah. This was the perspective expressed in b. Bava Metzia 59b. These traditions of the elders are to be obeyed merely because they are traditions of the elders. But Jesus does not wash his hands even while granting that it is a "tradition of the elders." And he implies that every human tradition must be measured against the commandment of God. Jesus therefore rejects the pretense to "presbyteral finality." The elders can never have the final say but must always be submitted to God's opinion as found in the written Torah. Their traditions are not binding merely as such and must even be disobeyed if they go contrary to God's commandment. The human word is only binding insofar as it succeeds in relating and bearing witness to the divine word.

Jesus's way of arguing likewise implies that God does not speak by means of the traditions of human beings. Otherwise the Pharisees would have the easy response that they are not preferring human traditions to God's commandments insofar as the two are not separable. The "finality" of the elders would be another way of referring to the finality of God. They could claim to be obeying God precisely by obeying the traditions of the elders. But Jesus disobeys their tradition of handwashing and says that they wrongly prefer human traditions to the commandments of God. This means that the human word is only binding insofar as it succeeds in relating and bearing witness to the divine word. One must therefore say that in Jesus's understanding human traditions are always one thing while the commandments of God are always another. One must distinguish between what God has said and what others pass on as an interpretation of God's words. Human theological traditions pretending to speak with God's authority can at most be attempts to relate and bear witness to what God has commanded, and these need not succeed simply as such or even when they have official sanction.

Jesus's argument still further implies that God does not exercise "dual agency" together with those who would speak for him. Otherwise the Pharisees would have the easy response of saying that they are in fact preferring the commandment of God precisely by obeying the traditions of human beings. The Pharisees could have claimed that there is not actually any contradiction between the commandment to honor parents and the rule about consecrating money to God because God speaks as much through the traditions of the elders themselves as through the written Torah.[13] And something similar could have been said in the case of the handwashing as

13. Compare Carson, "Matthew," 348.

well. That this tradition had arisen and become so commonplace could be taken as itself indicative of God's will; the traditions and their development are providentially guided. The idea of a "dual agency" would thus be a further way of making the human and divine words inseparable from each other: they would be inseparable precisely by really and effectively being one and the same word. Yet the divine word cannot be the measure for the human word unless the two are always separable and distinct in principle. One thing can be compared with another only if both things are distinctly and separately given. It makes no sense to compare a thing with itself. The Pharisees in John's Gospel admit this point when they complain: "You are testifying about yourself; your testimony is not true" (John 8:13). The truth of a claim must therefore be established by measuring it against something outside itself, and to say, as Jesus does, that human traditions must be subordinated to the word of God means therefore that God does not speak by means of the development and enshrinement of human traditions. The fact that some tradition has become commonplace or even widely accepted in the community of God's people does not entail that God means to endorse it. There is no such thing as "dual agency." There is always a certain "distance" between the divine speaker and the human speaker, so that the human word can do no more than to relate and bear witness to an original divine word.

It would be well now to summarize the point. Jesus neither acts nor argues like a "traditionalist." He disregards the official "tradition of the elders" about ritual handwashing before a meal and teaches his disciples to do the same. He likewise argues that the Pharisees' deference to their traditions put them in opposition to God's will. His polemics against the Pharisees can at first glance seem simplistic in light of the complex and various ways that the relationship between human traditions and divine words can be understood. There are many different ways from within the "traditionalist" paradigm for the Pharisees to justify themselves against Jesus's objection that they prefer human traditions to the commandments of God. But the simplicity of Jesus's arguments should perhaps instead be taken as itself indicating a fundamental difference of paradigm. It is not that he is arguing poorly but rather that he does not share their fundamentally "traditionalist" presuppositions. He does not grant the very assumptions which provide the Pharisees with their possible ways out of his argument. One can ask what these assumptions must be made for Jesus's argument to be as strong as possible. What must be presupposed in order for every avenue of response to be denied to the Pharisees? Elucidating these presuppositions will reveal that they are precisely such as entail the rejection of "traditionalism."

Jesus clearly denies that an officially sanctioned tradition in the community of God's people must be obeyed simply as such. It has no binding authority without a basis in a divine commandment; otherwise he would have ritually washed his hands before eating. He also clearly presupposes that every human word must be submitted to the divine word; otherwise he would not have complained that the Pharisees prefer human traditions to the divine commandment. But this imperative to compare the one to the other implies a conception according to which the human word is always separate and distinct from the divine word. Only separate and distinct things can be compared and subordinated one to the other in one's mind. One should thus think that God's speaking is always one thing while a human being's speaking is another. And these two presuppositions are critical. To say that the human word must always be submitted to the divine word is to reject the pretense to human "finality" which is characteristic of Pharisaic "traditionalism." No merely human authority is final and definitively binding; only God's word is final in matters of theology. He is the superior court of appeal in this field, and he has not granted such finality to anyone else. Jesus therefore feels no obligation to obey the tradition about handwashing. And to presuppose that the human and divine word are always distinct and separable is to reject the notion of "dual agency" by which the Roman Catholic pretense to magisterial infallibility can be understood. God does not speak by making use of the traditions of men the way one uses a knife to cut; otherwise certain human traditions could not be compared to the word of God but must simply be taken as being the manifestation of that word itself. This is why Jesus feels free not to engage in ritual handwashing. It is also why he feels free to object that the tradition about consecrating money goes contrary to the commandments to honor and not to curse one's parents. Jesus's understanding of human theological traditions is that they can at best be fallible and reversible attempts to relate and bear witness to what God has said. God speaks and commissions other persons to relate or write down what he has said. He does not simply speak through their speaking. There is always a certain unerasable "distance" between God and human beings which allows him always to be superior to them. They are never blended into one in the way that the notion of "dual agency" supposes.

These presuppositions of Jesus's argument are all ways of saying that every human word in theology is only ever derivatively authoritative as a fallible and reversible attempt to relate and bear witness to what God has said and done. But "traditionalism" admits that a human word can be strictly derivative while also being functionally original insofar as it is infallible and irreversible in principle: a word only ever spoken by a human being might nevertheless be rightly received as definitively as if it had come from the mouth of God himself. Jesus does not accept this. It therefore follows from this that Jesus rejects "traditionalism."

QUESTIONS AND MISCONCEPTIONS

It would be well at this point to consider some possible confusions and mis-
conceptions that may arise in response to the idea that Jesus rejects "traditionalism." Some of these points will be addressed in greater detail later on.
But it may be worthwhile to provide some brief answers here.

Does the denial of "traditionalism" mean that there is no principle of
identity in the church as Jesus's messianic community? Does it mean there is
nothing to serve as the unifying foundation of his followers? No.

The denial of "traditionalism" means that no one generation of the
group can make a decision about some matter of practice or belief that is
definitive and binding for all later generations. Those in the future are not
necessarily beholden to the opinions and convictions of those in the past.
The group can reform itself or develop in new directions. Jesus thus did not
believe that his disciples had to obey the traditions of the elders whom the
Pharisees so venerated. But this does not mean that they have nothing in
common or that there is nothing to the identity of the group beyond what
any one generation determines. What they have in common is a shared orientation toward Jesus as their common teacher in whom they believe. Every
generation of Christians has always tried to be faithful to him. It is always
possible for one to manage to do this better than another in some respects,
but what makes them all to be generations of one and the same body or
group is this shared orientation toward Jesus their teacher from whom they
all wish to learn.

The following image may be helpful in understanding this point. Aristotle, Ptolemy, Nicolaus Copernicus, Isaac Newton, and Albert Einstein
all believed radically different things. One thinker's theories were rejected
and replaced with another's. This other's theories were influential and even
considered definitive until they came to be supplanted by yet another's. This
is the way things go. Human beings are not born knowing everything but
rather must learn over time. And yet Aristotle, Ptolemy, Copernicus, Newton, and Einstein were all members of this body of human beings called
"scientists." What made them all to be scientists, despite the radical differences between their opinions, is the fact that they shared a common orientation toward the world of nature. Each one was fascinated by this world and
attempted to understand it better by means of the methods and insights
available to him in his time. Each was in a genuine contact with one and the
same natural reality which provided for all and had more than enough room
for every one of them. Their identity as scientists is founded in their shared
interest in and orientation toward the world that they had in common

rather than in their particular scientific opinions. Each one wanted to be a student of nature.

This is also a useful image for understanding the church. It is the society of Jesus's followers and would-be students. What makes each generation of Christians to be a part of one and the same body is that they share a common orientation and loyalty toward Jesus from whom they would learn how to live as God's people in the world. Each one wants to be a student of Jesus the teacher, and they can have this shared orientation even if the practices and beliefs of one generation are very different from those of another. They can have this shared orientation even if one generation looks radically different from the ones that came before it.

Does the rejection of "traditionalism" mean that there is no place for a healthy respect for tradition in the church? Must every generation start from scratch and recreate the faith in its own way? No.

The first thing to say is that such a situation is not even possible in principle. For example, scientists are not born but rather made. Students must first be taught the dominant theories by persons who are already scientists. Only then can they make theoretical adjustments or propose alternative theories in accordance with their convictions about the data. No scientific understanding is possible at all without a preliminary education or initiation into an existing tradition of inquiry. The same thing is true also in theology. No one is born a Christian. Every generation of the church must first receive the faith from the one that comes before it. Only then can it make the adjustments it deems necessary. No one can even understand the things that theology talks about without being taught about them by other persons who already inhabit a particular tradition. The idea that every generation starts from scratch in constructing its own conception of the faith is consequently impossible to realize.

The following analogy could prove helpful. Consider how a person cannot see things without a power of sight. It is one's power of sight that makes things visible to one, and things are only visible to one as far as this power of sight allows. Things may look blurry to a person, not because they are themselves blurry but rather because he or she has poor vision. Or consider how a person cannot understand a text without an ability to read. One's reading knowledge of a language is analogous to one's sense of sight in that it is what makes it possible for a particular type of object—namely, texts—to appear to one with clarity. Something similar is true in the faith as well. One cannot even begin to think about the faith and to wrestle with it without first being taught it by another. One must be introduced to the notions of "God," "Jesus," "faith," "salvation," "sin," and the rest. One must be given definitions and stipulations of what these words means so that expressions of the faith in Scripture or other sources can be intelligible. And the name for this process of receiving the faith from another is precisely "tradition."[14]

This means that "tradition" as a general phenomenon is inevitable and necessary, since a way of life is always passed down (*tradere*) from one person to another. But it is another matter altogether for the church to operate by means of "traditionalism." One must recall that "traditionalism" as the term is being used here refers to a very specific idea. It does not really have much to do with "tradition" as a general and universal phenomenon. It is rather the idea that one generation of a group at a certain point in time can make a definitive and binding decision about some matter of practice or belief on pain of exclusion from the group. It is the idea that the members of a group at one point in time can legitimately and definitively determine that certain practices or beliefs will or will not constitute the identity of the group from that moment forward. This imposes a "traditionalist" mentality on future generations of this group insofar as their belonging to a group with a coherent identity requires their allegiance to the particular opinions of a past generation. The rejection of this idea does not mean that there is no place for tradition in the church. There would not be a church at all if there were no tradition, since every person is made a Christian through the handing-on (*traditio*) of the faith by another. The rejection of "traditionalism" only means that there is no one generation's tradition so binding and definitive as to be invulnerable to questioning or reversal by a later generation in their sincere attempt better to understand what Jesus teaches.

It is also worth noting once more that Jesus does not practice ritual handwashing before a meal despite the fact that this is a "tradition of the elders." This tradition of course has no grounding in a divine commandment. God never demanded that the Jewish people as a whole to do it. It is rather a part of the "oral Torah" and not the written Torah. Therefore it is not binding. It is true that Jesus does not teach against it. He does not command that a person specifically not wash his or her hands before eating. But he certainly does not feel obligated to observe it either. He does not grant the "traditions of the elders" normative force. Ritual handwashing or some other such tradition may be something one may do if one feels so inclined, but it is not the sort of thing that one can oblige others to do. This is apparently because God himself does not oblige it. Jesus thus implicitly acknowledges limits to the normativity of traditions. It is not that traditions must all be rejected, but rather that a tradition cannot be forced upon others

14. See O'Collins, *Tradition*.

simply because it is a tradition of whatever official endorsement. Only what God or Jesus demands can be demanded of others.

There is the following text: "Therefore, brothers, stand firm and cling to the traditions that you learned, either by word of mouth or by our epistle" (2 Thess 2:15). Paul refers to the things that the Thessalonians received from him as "traditions." He does so rightly because this is exactly what they are: things handed down (*traditiones*) from one person to another. But to suppose that this text supports "traditionalism" is a *non sequitur*. Paul does not say that anything that commends itself with the title "tradition" is worth keeping. Jesus himself did not keep the "tradition of the elders" (Matt 15:2/ Mark 7:2–3). The point in the argument above was not that Jesus has an allergy to the notion of "tradition" simply as such. Neither is it any response to show that the New Testament speaks of traditions or that "the Gospel . . . itself is to be treated as tradition—that is, literally, 'that which is handed down.'" Such is Peter Kreeft's misinterpretation of the argument.[15] The point is something else altogether: that traditions as such—things a person says or passes on to others—are not unconditionally binding unless they are the words of God. And Paul is not referring to tradition as a general category but to the specific teachings that were passed on to the Thessalonians. These particular teachings (which were perhaps about the coming of Christ: 2 Thess 2:1–12; cf. 1 Thess 4:13–5:11) are what must be kept. It is thus one thing to say that one must hold fast to particular traditions and another altogether to say that one must hold fast to "traditions" simply as such. Some things handed down are to be kept, but not everything is to be kept simply because it is handed down.

Does the rejection of "traditionalism" mean that any theological opinion or interpretation of Jesus's teaching is as good as any other? Does it lead into a kind of total relativism in which there is no true and false? No.

Consider once more the analogy of science. Contemporary science does not function by means of "traditionalism." No single generation of scientists can determine for all time that a particular theory is to be held or practice to be followed. The dominant scientific paradigms of today could be rejected tomorrow; what is now popular could later be discredited. Yet this by itself does not mean that there is not a difference between true and false in science. The same principle holds in theology. It is not always easy to tell what exactly the proper interpretation of a certain idea or teaching of Jesus might be. The popular understanding of one generation can be rejected by another. But this does not mean that there is no true or false. It is just that the sense of the truth in one generation of a group can be different than in

15. Kreeft, "Why?," 135.

another. There is nevertheless a single standard of truth against which every generation is measured: the teaching of Jesus itself.

Truth and tradition relate to each other in a certain way. Consider how a physical object can only be viewed from some point of view or other. There is no view from nowhere. And yet, as the phenomenologist Maurice Merleau-Ponty notes, certain points of view can be better than others for revealing those aspects or dimensions of an object with which one is interested.[16] Every point of view makes some things visible and hides others; what is hidden from one position may become clear from another. One can change one's point of view in order to get a better look at the thing and to see what one is interested in seeing about it. The same thing is true in the case of theology. It is true that one cannot understand Jesus's teachings at all without first being initiated into a particular tradition. One must be given a set of prior notions and preconceptions about what certain words can mean and how they can be used by which one can make sense of what is written in the biblical texts. But it is also possible to make adjustments to that tradition if it should prove incapable of making sense of certain things that Jesus teaches. It could be that certain critical assumptions of this idea make it unnecessarily difficult or strained to interpret what Jesus says at times. Thomas Joseph White thus is correct: "The realistic question is not whether we will have a tradition, but which one are we to have."[17] One can change one's tradition just as one might change one's perspective in order to get a better view of one's object of concern.

G. L. Prestige gives the following analogy. He compares the apostolic testimony to Jesus and creeds formulated later as summarizing that testimony to evidence and verdict:

> The Gospels afford a collection of material for theological construction; the creed puts forward inferences and conclusions based on that material. The one represents the evidence, the other records a verdict. And be that verdict ever so correct, the fact remains that it was the evidence, and not the formal verdict, which was once deposited with the saints.[18]

And from this it follows that it is in principle "always open to review that evidence afresh."[19] This is precisely what the rejection of "traditionalism" amounts to. The "official" conclusions endorsed by one generation need not be accepted by a later one.

16. Merleau-Ponty, *Phenomenology of Perception*, 315–16.
17. White, *Light of Christ*, 35.
18. Prestige, *Fathers and Heretics*, 7.
19. Prestige, *Fathers and Heretics*, 7.

These remarks should help to clarify what Jesus's rejection of "traditionalism" does and does not mean. It does mean that every person apart from him exercises theological authority in a derivative, fallible, and in principle reversible manner. It does mean that the church of today is not necessarily beholden to the same opinions, concerns, and attitudes of the church of yesterday—if the teachings of Jesus do not demand this. But it does not mean that there is no principle of unity in the church at all. This principle of unity is Jesus the Teacher from whom all Christians wish to learn. What makes it to be one church is that everyone within it is turned toward Jesus in the hope of learning from him. The unity of the church emerges from this shared orientation of the heart among all Christians. Neither does it mean that there is no room for tradition at all in Christian theology. It is impossible to become a Christian or to engage in theology without first being initiated into a particular tradition by someone else who already inhabits it. Neither does it mean that there is no truth or falsity in theology. Jesus's teachings themselves are the measure of every interpretation of them, just as nature itself is the measure of every scientific theory about it. Any tradition can be rejected or modified if doing so makes it possible to understand Jesus's teachings more accurately.

SUMMARY OF THE ARGUMENT

The argument of this chapter can therefore be summarized as follows. Jesus should be interpreted as rejecting the "traditionalism" of the Pharisees. He does not accept that the words of mere humans can be used as "tools" for exercising theological authority. Otherwise there are too many obvious responses to be given on behalf of the Pharisees to his polemics. His arguments against them are strong and convincing only if he is interpreted from the point of view of certain "anti-traditionalist" presuppositions and thus as rejecting the "traditionalist" paradigm altogether.

Jesus rejects the idea that a present generation of the people of God is necessarily beholden to the practices and beliefs that were of central concern to past generations. He exemplifies this attitude himself when he and his disciples do not ritually wash their hands before eating in accordance with the traditions of the elders, and he likewise rejects the Pharisees' teaching about consecrating money to God instead of caring for one's parents. This is because Jesus believes that every human tradition must be measured against the commandments of God. This means that God has not provided human beings with the kind of "finality" that the Pharisees presumed the traditions of the elders to have. One is never unconditionally obliged to obey other human beings in the matter of one's friendship with God. But this work of subordinating and comparing the human word to the divine word also presupposes that the words of human beings are always separable and distinct from the words of God. There can be no comparing things that effectively blend into each other. This consequently entails that human traditions are not themselves God's speech but rather at best attempts to bear witness to that speech. God speaks from his own mouth and human beings have the responsibility of testifying truthfully to what he has said. There is no "dual agency"; there is no promise of providential guidance. The word of God is always one thing and human traditions another. The two may agree, but they never become inseparable from one another. These are the necessary presuppositions of Jesus's argumentation against the Pharisees. And they entail that Jesus rejects "traditionalism." As Adolf von Harnack said: "[T]he Gospel knows absolutely nothing of intercourse with God being bound up with reverence for tradition itself."[20]

---

20. Harnack, *What is Christianity?*, 228.

4

Against "Hierarchy"

"HIERARCHY" IS THE IDEA that a particular community is intrinsically structured in such a way that certain persons within it have the right and standing in principle to demand things of others without opening themselves up to correction or legitimate refusal. Not everyone is on a par. Some persons enjoy an unconditional authority that others do not, and the power of some is occasionally not counterbalanced by that of others. It is a further dimension of a "high" view of ecclesial authority in theology. The question in the present chapter is whether "hierarchy" describes Jesus's understanding of the church as his messianic community.

BROTHERS AND STUDENTS OF THE MESSIAH

Jesus very clearly claims such a privilege for himself. It would be tedious to provide every bit of textual evidence available. For example, he says: "All things have been handed over to me by my Father, and no one knows the Son except the Father, and no one knows the Father except the Son and the one to whom the Son wishes to reveal him" (Matt 11:27). No one else apart from the Son is capable of knowing or revealing the Father, so that no one else can say what the Father does or does not want from human beings. The Son therefore has ultimate theological authority. No one can correct him or call him into question because no one knows the Father apart from him. It is on the basis of his unique knowledge of God the Father that he can call all people to learn from him: "Come to me, all you who are weary and burdened, and I will give you rest" (v. 28). And elsewhere he says: "I am the

26

light of the world. Whoever follows me will never walk in darkness but will have the light of life" (John 8:12). Jesus is thus not one light among others but rather the very light of the world. And he tells the Pharisees: "You know neither me nor my Father. If you knew me, you would know my Father also" (v. 19). Jesus binds himself and his identity with that of his Father. One cannot be known without the other. He thus certainly claims the right and standing to command things of others without opening himself up to questioning or correction in virtue of his privileged knowledge of God the Father. John Bowker summarizes the "offense" of Jesus to his interlocutors as follows: "Fundamentally, the offense of Jesus . . . lay in his attitude toward the various sources of authority, since in many different ways he claimed and exemplified direct authority, and power, from God."[1] And Adolf von Harnack summarizes the idea by saying that "this Jesus who preached humility and knowledge of self, nevertheless named himself and himself alone as the Son of God. He is certain that he knows the Father, that he is to bring this knowledge to all men, and that thereby he is doing the work of God."[2]

But a closer reading of the New Testament further reveals that Jesus does not grant functionally this same authority to anyone else. This is especially evident in what he says toward the beginning of a blistering anti-Pharisaical diatribe in the Gospel according to Matthew:

> You are not to be called "rabbi," for you all have one teacher while you are all brothers. And do not call anyone on earth your "father," for you all have one Father in the heavens. Neither are you to be called instructors, for the Messiah alone is your instructor (23:8–10).

These commands addressed to his disciples are very provocative, but it is important not to get distracted by facile and confused misreadings of Jesus's words here. He very clearly does not principally have in mind the mere use of certain titles to describe certain persons within the community of his followers. He will later refer to the "prophets, sages, and scribes" (v. 34) to be sent by him whom the Pharisees will kill. These are even loftier titles than "rabbi," "father," and "instructor." Paul also would later say that Jesus left "teachers" in the church (Eph 4:11). And he elsewhere says that he became a "father" to the Corinthians whom he evangelized (1 Cor 4:15). Presumably he does not mean to contradict Jesus—although it is admittedly one thing to describe a person as a teacher or as a figurative "father" and it is quite another to adopt those words as titles. The mere use of certain words is

---

1. Bowker, *Jesus and the Pharisees*, 42.
2. Harnack, *What is Christianity?*, 129.

therefore irrelevant to Jesus's point. He is not forbidding his disciples from ever uttering the word "father" or "instructor" with respect to other persons. Neither does he mean to say that it would be illegitimate for children to address their male parents by the name "father," which would be ridiculous. All such considerations are entirely irrelevant to the real point that he means to be making.

These commands must be interpreted as a part of Jesus's larger rejection of the very system of religion of the "scribes and Pharisees, hypocrites" (Matt 23:13) in the whole of Matthew's Gospel and especially in the diatribe of this particular chapter. They are not trivial rules about words with so many obvious counterexamples that in the end, after a hundred qualifications are made, they end up saying nothing. The teachings are more substantial than that. As Craig Blomberg writes: "[S]uch titles [as Jesus prohibits] are not to be used to confer privilege or status."[3] This point can be explained as follows.

What Jesus means to say is that he and God the Father alone exercise theological authority in an original, infallible, and in principle irreversible way. God and Jesus alone are unconditional and unquestionable theological authorities in the church. All other persons at most exercise the derivative authority of fallibly and in principle reversibly relating and bearing witness to his teachings and the works of God in him. R. T. France comments that: "[I]n relation to [Jesus] all his followers stand on an equal footing as brothers. Jesus thus incidentally asserts his own unique authority: he has the only true claim to 'Moses' seat.'"[4] The rejection of titles is thus not an implausible complaint about mere words but rather serves the greater purpose of maintaining the clear boundary and "distance" in matters of theological authority between God and Jesus on one side and all Christian disciples on the other. One is not to use certain titles for others, nor to accept them for oneself, precisely so as to avoid thinking or being thought of in such a way that the fundamental distinction between God/Jesus and everyone else in matters of theological authority is blurred. Consider the matter point by point.

The Pharisees believed that the commandments of God had to be interpreted and kept in light of the officially sanctioned decisions of teachers of past generations. These teachers were set up by God in a position of authority and could "bind" and "loose" as they saw fit. Human teachers and God were thus functionally on a par. Disobedience to the one was disobedience to the other. But Jesus thought that the Pharisees' commitment to the preoccupations of their predecessors and prior teachers—specifically in the

---

3. Blomberg, *Matthew*, 343.

4. France, *Gospel according to Matthew*, 325.

matters of ritual purity[5]—led them not to understand the true meaning of God's commandment. This comes out in their objecting to his dining with sinners or his disciples' eating grain from the fields on the Sabbath. He tells them they have lost sight of what God said: "I desire mercy and not sacrifice" (Hos 6:6; Matt 9:13, 12:7). God does not want ritual purity but rather the healing, harmony, and reconciliation of human beings with God and with each other. As David Garland comments: "What matters to God is not ritual observance and ethical behavior, but ethical behavior alone."[6] The people from whom the Pharisees learned thus did not teach them how to understand God's word rightly. This is why Jesus insists that he alone is the "teacher" and "instructor" of his followers. His disciples are neither to consider themselves to be teachers of anyone nor to accept that others call them teachers in any special sense. Their own words must always be measured against the words of Jesus, and they have no further authorization than that of relating and bearing witness to his teachings. This is how Jesus works to prevent past generation of teachers from leading future generations down the wrong path.

The Pharisees also showed respect and deference to earlier teachers of the Law whom they called "fathers."[7] There was no obedience to God that was not also an obedience to them. God was inseparable from these "fathers." This same linguistic practice exists in "traditionalist" forms of Christianity as well. One reads of references to the "church fathers" or "holy fathers." The Council of Chalcedon defined its doctrine of Christ by saying: "we follow the Holy Fathers in all things."[8] One even finds Roman Catholic writers arguing that "the Fathers know best."[9] God and human figures from the past thus blur into one and become inseparable. But Jesus insists that one is not to speak this way about others. God alone is "Father." The philosopher Michel Henry calls this "the substitution of a divine genealogy for a natural genealogy."[10] One's relationship to God, who is the source of one's life and of all things, is essentially not a matter of submitting reverentially and as if unconditionally to certain merely human teachers. Jesus gives an enacted example of this distinction between God and all human predecessors when he ignores the tradition about ritual handwashing before a meal. Jesus's disciples are not to confuse their relationship to God their Father with a

---

5. See Bowker, *Jesus and the Pharisees*, 16–17, 44–45.

6. Garland, *Reading Matthew*, 164.

7. Carson, "Matthew," 475.

8. Cited in McGuckin, *Orthodox Church*, 149.

9. Akin, *Fathers Know Best*.

10. Henry, *Words of Christ*, 41; emphasis removed.

kind of deferential loyalty to certain significant figures from the past. They do not lose God simply because they disobey the traditions of the elders venerated by the Pharisees, because God is separable and accessible apart from the mere human persons who bear witness to him. God as Father of all is equally proximate to everyone and accessible to every person through faith.[11] Every person in the church therefore must be clearly distinguished from God who is above all.

The Pharisees likewise presumed for themselves the right to interpret the Law in a way that is binding and definitive. They believed they had the right to become teachers and fathers for the present as well as later generations of Jews. But Jesus maintains to the contrary that his followers are all simply students in the classroom of the Messiah. He is their one instructor. All his disciples are equal in rank in comparison with each other; no one of them is above the others. Robert Gundry comments that they are in a position of "equality of subjection to Jesus's didactic authority."[12] Anything that any other person proposes therefore can and must always be measured against the standard of Jesus's own teachings. The goal is always to learn from Jesus himself and not simply from this or that student of his.

Jesus consequently insists sharply on a "distance" between God the Father and himself on one side and all his disciples in the church on the other. This is why titles and the use of certain forms of language are rejected: to maintain a sense of the differentiation and separation between God and Jesus and all mere humans. The rule about words is founded upon a difference in authority which the rejection of the use of certain titles is supposed to reflect. God and Jesus alone are unquestionable authorities. Thus D. A. Carson: "[T]he risen Christ is as displeased with those in his church who demand unquestioning submission to themselves and their opinions and confuse a reputation for showy piety with godly surrender to his teaching as he was with any Pharisee."[13]

It was mentioned earlier that "traditionalism" and "hierarchy" are closely related ideas. The presumption to define the identity of a group in a binding and definitive way is fortified when it is connected to the occupant of a particular rank within the hierarchy of the community. The presumption to possess unquestionable and uncorrectable authority within a group is clarified when one can determine the essential identity of the group in a binding and definitive way. One idea thus supports the other. It therefore should not go unnoticed that one and the same principle asserted by Jesus

11. Bowker, *Jesus and the Pharisees*, 52.

12. Gundry, *Matthew*, 457.

13. Carson, "Matthew," 475.

implies the rejection of both "traditionalism" and "hierarchy" alike. More specifically, to say that all human words must be measured against the divine word is to exclude both ideas. It excludes "traditionalism" because it means that all human words are only derivatively, fallibly, and reversibly authoritative in principle. They are at best attempts to relate and bear witness to the divine word. And it excludes "hierarchy" for the same reason. There is no one in the church apart from God and Jesus who cannot be questioned or corrected in principle. Everyone in the church is but a "brother" and fellow student of the Messiah as the one true Teacher. This means that everyone in the church as the classroom of the Messiah can in principle be questioned or corrected by another. And from this it follows that Jesus rejects "hierarchy" as applied to his followers.

This rejection of "hierarchy" is consonant with Jesus's teachings about service. His disciples dispute amongst themselves about who is greatest (Luke 22:24). He rebukes them and teaches that they must have a change of mentality: "The kings of the Gentiles lord it over them, and those in authority over them are called benefactors. But you all should not be like this. Instead, the greatest among you must become like the youngest, and the leader like a servant" (vv. 25–26). His teaching is thus that his disciples must act in such a way as not to call attention to any hierarchical distinctions among them. David Turner thus writes: "Jesus's egalitarianism . . . frees his disciples to live in a community where humble reciprocal service rules."[14] And Garland: "The church that is envisioned is egalitarian with the only ranks being brother, sister (12:50, 28:10), and servant. Equality, not elitism, is its mark of distinction."[15]

This is not to say that there are no differences among them at all. Some are "greater" while others are "younger." Some are "leaders" while others are "servants." Some are granted tasks or appointments that others are not. Some persons are more prominent than others in terms of gifting and ability or even simply as a matter of personality. It is impossible that there be no differences at all among a variety of persons within a single group. But what Jesus teaches is that these differences must not be emphasized or brought into relief in such a manner as to imply "hierarchy." The paradigmatic manifestation of "hierarchy" is the presumption of an unquestionable and uncorrectable authority, yet Jesus does not grant to anyone else this sort of privilege. He therefore directs his disciples' attention away from the question of their comparative greatness to the more fitting preoccupation of mutual service.

14. Turner, *Matthew*, 548.

15. Garland, *Reading Matthew*, 234.

One might wonder whether this reading is quite so plausible. Jesus proceeds just after this moment in Luke's Gospel to tell his disciples the following lofty words:

> You are the ones who have remained with me in my trials. And I confer my kingdom on you just as my Father conferred it on me, so that you may eat and drink at my table in my kingdom, and you will sit on thrones judging the twelve tribes of Israel (Luke 22:28–30).

Jesus uttered these words to the eleven disciples. It is not something that he said to just anyone and everyone. The image of the disciples sitting on thrones and judging the twelve tribes of Israel thus might seem strongly to imply a kind of "hierarchical" differentiation between the apostles and everyone else within the world or at least the messianic community of the church. The apostles thus appear to have been granted a special authority in Jesus's kingdom that is not granted to just anyone else, and a special authority could be taken as implying the right and standing to expect unquestioned, uncontested obedience from others. From this it would appear to follow that Jesus does not in fact deny "hierarchy" in the church. The apostles might seem the paradigmatic example of "hierarchical" figures.

This line of argumentation may seem initially plausible, yet it does not change the fact that Jesus told his disciples clearly in Matthew's Gospel: "You are all brothers and students of the one Teacher that is the Messiah." One could be tempted to say that Matthew and Luke have differing conceptions of authority and hierarchy within the church, but it would be better to find a way of reading this text from Luke's Gospel consistently with the thesis supported by Matthew's text that Jesus rejects "hierarchy" in the church. And such a reading is in fact possible.

Jesus's language is figurative. The eleven will not "sit on thrones" and "judge the twelve tribes of Israel" in the sense of being established in an exclusive and privileged position of authority within Jesus's church. This, too, would be a figurative reading, but it is not the figurative reading being proposed here. The apostles will rather be preaching the gospel of the risen Jesus and disrupting the order of things in Israel as they open up the kingdom of heaven to those who accept their preaching while closing it to others who reject it. They sit on thrones and judge the twelve tribes when for example they preach the resurrection to Jews from all around at Pentecost (Acts 2) or when they refuse to submit to the Council's command that they stop preaching in the name of Jesus (Acts 4–5). The "thrones" and "judgment" are therefore metaphors and images describing the activity of the twelve as related by Luke in the Acts of the Apostles.[16] They exercise theological authority without being distinguished from any others according to rank within a hierarchy; they are sharing in Jesus's "kingdom" and sitting on a "throne" within it because they preach his authoritative word to others.

This alternative reading may not seem totally compelling now. It is certainly possible but perhaps not convincing. But the matter will become clearer if attention is turned to other passages in which the problem of apostolic authority is even more explicitly discussed. The notorious words of Jesus to Simon at Matt 16:17–19 will prove most relevant. The central question is the following: In what does apostolic authority consist and how is it exercised? It will be argued that the theological authority of the apostles (as of all Christians whatsoever) is no more than the derivative authority of relating and bearing witness to the teachings of Jesus and the works of God in him to others and of interpreting them in a fallible and in principle reversible manner.

ON THIS ROCK

Jesus asks his disciples who people thought the Son of Man was. They respond by naming the various beliefs that one could find among the Jews at that time: John the Baptist, Elijah, Jeremiah, or another of the prophets. Jesus then asks his disciples who they think he is. Simon responds by affirming: "You are the Messiah, the Son of the living God" (Matt 16:16). Jesus then tells him:

> Blessed are you, Simon bar Jonah, for flesh and blood has not revealed [this] to you but my Father in the heavens. And I say to you that you are Peter [*Petros*], and on this rock [*petra*] I will build my church, and the gates of Hades will not prevail against it [*autēs*]. I will give you the keys of the kingdom of heaven, and whatever you bind on earth will have been bound in heaven, and whatever you loose on earth will have been loosed in heaven (vv. 17–19).

Donald Hagner has described this as being among the most controversial passages in theological history.[17] It raises a number of controverted questions.

A common reading found among Roman Catholic interpreters is as follows.[18] Simon Peter (*Petros*) is singled out as the rock (*petra*) on which

---

16. See Wenkel, "When the Apostles Became Kings."

17. Hagner, *Matthew 14–28*, 469.

18. See Mitch and Sri, *Gospel of Matthew*, 207–10 for a representative example. A

Jesus will build a church that will prevail over the gates of Hades. The claim is that *Petros* means the same thing as *petra*. Therefore the terms both refer to Simon himself. Jesus says to him: "You are (the) Rock and on this rock." He is uniquely given the "keys" of the kingdom of heaven together with the special privilege of "binding" and "loosing" in a guaranteed accordance with the will of heaven. He is thus being promised the same kind of "finality" that the Pharisees presumed for themselves and for the teachings of the elders. One could also suppose that Jesus promises Simon that he will be the beneficiary of God's "dual agency." He will bind or loose what will have already been bound or loosed in heaven in the sense that God will bind or loose on earth through Simon himself. This is therefore both a "traditional-ist" and "hierarchical" reading of the passage. The church will be built upon Simon himself, his determinations to bind or loose will remain binding and definitive for all subsequent generations, and this "finality" associated with them will or at least could be grounded in the "dual agency" he will exercise with God binding and loosing through him.

Ludwig Ott among contemporary Roman Catholic theologians sum-marizes the interpretation very well as follows:

> Christ made Peter the foundation of his Church, that is, the guarantor of her unity and unshakable strength, and promised her a duration that will not pass away (Mt. 16, 18). However, the unity and solidity of the Church is not possible without the right Faith. Peter is, therefore, also the supreme teacher of the Faith. As such he must be infallible in the official promulgation of Faith, in his own person and in his successors since by Christ's decree the Church is to continue for all time. Again, Christ be-stowed on Peter (and on his successors) a comprehensive power of binding and loosing. As in Rabbinical speech one understood by binding and loosing also the authentic [i.e., authoritative] declaration of the law, so the power is also contained therein of authentically declaring the law of the New Covenant, the Gospel. God in Heaven will confirm the Pope's judgment. This supposes that, in his capacity of supreme Doctor of the Faith, he is preserved from error.[19]

Matthew Levering likewise defends the Roman Catholic doctrine of the papacy in the same way on the basis of this very passage.[20] And Peter Kreeft

---

number of Roman Catholic apologists have also been advocating for this reading at the semipopular level in recent times. See the discussions in Akin, *Teaching with Authority*; Heschmeyer, *Pope Peter*; Horn, *Case for Catholicism*; and Ray, *Upon This Rock*.

19. Ott, *Fundamentals of Catholic Dogma*, 287.

20. Levering, *Was the Reformation a Mistake?*, ch. 9.

writes that his suspicion of an unjust claim to power on the part of the pope was undone by this passage: "Christ did bestow on Peter the name of 'Rock,' and the keys of the kingdom, and the promise that the church he founded on that rock would conquer hell."[21]

There would be very much to say by way of response.[22] The idea in brief will be that it is both possible and desirable to read this passage differently. A number of arguments will be presented for this conclusion. The first matter to address is the identity of the *petra* on which the church is built. Does this refer to Simon *Petros*? Or maybe rather to Jesus himself? The argument will be made here that it refers to Jesus and not to Simon.

Even many Protestant commentators agree that Simon is the *petra*.[23] Chrys Caragounis notes that this position has become a sort of consensus among scholars.[24] In the ancient world, this reading of things was proposed by Pope Leo the Great (*Letters* 10). Ambrose of Milan also agrees with it (*Exposition of the Christian Faith* 4.57). But it is possible to show that the grammar of the sentence itself does not demand that *Petros* and *petra* refer to the same thing. It rather suggests against this idea. This conclusion follows whether *Petros* is applied to Simon as a proper name or else as a common noun, likewise whether one says that *petros* is synonymous with *petra* or not.

Suppose for the moment that *Petros* is applied to Simon as a proper name. It would therefore follow that Jesus is not calling Simon a rock.[25] Naming a person is not the same thing as calling them a something or other. The name "Andrew" means brave and manly, but this does not mean that all parents who name their son "Andrew" are calling him manly and brave. He is after all only a baby when he receives his name! This is made even more obvious when one considers that most names have a feminine form as well. Parents are hardly calling their infant daughters "brave and manly" by naming them "Andrea" or some such equivalent. Neither are parents necessarily calling their children "lovers of horses" by naming them "Philip" or "Philippa." The lesson is therefore clear. Jesus's application of *Petros* to Simon as a proper name simply would not mean straightaway that he is calling Simon a rock. It would mean rather that he is calling him "Peter" (*Petros*). And

21. Kreeft, "Why?," 132.

22. See especially the critical discussion in Caragounis, *Peter and the Rock*.

23. Blomberg, *Matthew*, 251–52; Carson, "Matthew," 368; France, *Gospel according to Matthew*, 254–55; Talbert, *Matthew*, 195; Turner, *Matthew*, 404.

24. Caragounis, *Peter and the Rock*, 1.

25. Contrary to Mitch and Sri, *Gospel of Matthew*, 207.

Caragounis has compiled evidence that suggests that it need not have been a previously unknown name in the ancient Greek and Latin world.[26]

It is true that *Petros* resembles *petra*. Jesus's application of the name to him could therefore be taken as implying that Simon bears some relation to the *petra* on which the church will be built. But this does not require that Simon is himself that *petra*. Consider how the name "Theodore" means "gift of God." A person can live up to the meaning of this name if he acts in such a way as to prove to be a gift to those around him. Or consider how the name "Andrew" means "brave and manly." A person can live up to the meaning of that name by doing something brave and manly. Something similar might therefore be happening here. Simon can be called *Petros* by Jesus because he lives up to the meaning or significance of that name. But what is that meaning?

There is no necessity in saying that Simon is *Petros* in the sense of being himself the *petra* on which the church is built. It could be rather that Simon is being told that he lives up to the name of *Petros* because he is "of (the) *petra*." He is not "the rock" or even "a rock" but rather "rock" or "rocky" or "of (the) rock." His confession of Jesus as the Messiah and Son of the living God puts him in a special relation to the *petra* on which the church is built. He is made of the same stuff (so to speak); he becomes *Petros* because he confesses the *petra*; he is *Petros* because by the recognition of Jesus's true identity he is built upon the *petra* (cf. 7:24–25). Consider how one could say that a house "participates" or "shares" derivatively in the original stability of its foundation. Simon thus becomes *Petros* in a derivative way in the light of his confessing Jesus the original *petra*. This means that the name *Petros* as applied to Simon would function more like an adjective than a noun. It communicates that Simon is related to the *petra* in a certain way rather than being himself a *petra*; it is describing him adjectivally in relation to the *petra*. This is in fact the reading that Augustine gives. He writes that Simon is named "Peter" after Jesus the *petra* without himself being that *petra*, just as "Christians" are named after Christ and not Christ after Christians (*Sermons on the New Testament* 26.1–2). The name "Christian" expresses a relation on the part of its bearer to Christ; so also *Petros* communicates a relation on the part of Simon to the *petra*. There is therefore nothing about *Petros* as applied to Simon as a proper name that demands that he is also the *petra* on which the church is built.

But suppose instead that *petros* is applied to Simon as a common noun. It is not that he is being named "Peter," but rather that he is being called "a *petros*." The next question to ask would therefore be whether *petros* and *petra* are synonymous or not.

26. Caragounis, *Peter and the Rock*, 17–25.

Assume that *petros* and *petra* as common nouns are synonymous. This is the opinion of some commentators like Carson, Craig Evans, and Curtis Mitch and Edward Sri.[27] Caragounis writes that "not only in classical but also in biblical Greek no clear-cut distinction can be made between [*petra*] and [*petros*]."[28] The two words are both Greek nouns that can mean "rock." It must be noted then that accepting this synonymy makes it inexplicable why Matthew would use two different words in such close succession to refer to Simon in both cases. He could easily have written: "You are a *petros* and on this *petros*."[29] Or he could have written: "You are the *petra* and on this *petra*." Certainly the fact that *petra* is grammatically feminine does not mean that Simon could not be called "the *petra*." He is just as easily called a neuter *skandalon* ("stumbling block") not long after this (16:23), and Jesus himself is called "the *petra*" by Paul (1 Cor 10:4). There is thus no reason why Matthew could not have used the same word twice if indeed he understood Jesus to be referring to Simon in both cases.

Some scholars will claim that Jesus would have been speaking in Aramaic to Simon in this episode as follows: "You are *kepha* and on this *kepha*."[30] One and the same word would thus have been used first as a proper name and then as a common noun. Joseph Ratzinger appeals to this point on the basis of various Semiticisms discernible in the text in order to defend the notion of Petrine primacy.[31] But this hypothetical original double use of *kepha* can be called into question. Caragounis argues: "While we know that [*kepha*] underlies [*Petros*], we have no way of knowing which Aramaic word underlines [*petra*]."[32] This is because there are two Aramaic words that correspond to the Greek *petra*, namely *kepha* and *tinarah*, and it is impossible to determine which word would have been used in this hypothetical Aramaic original phrase.[33] Furthermore, it is worth mentioning that this reading takes for granted that Simon must be the referent of *petra*. That is why it asserts that *kepha* would have been used twice instead of just once. But this is precisely what needs to be proved! It cannot simply be assumed. The question to be answered is why Simon must be the referent of *petra*. This appeal to a hypothetical Aramaic original is thus circular.

27. Carson, "Matthew," 368; Evans, *Matthew*, 313; Mitch and Sri, *Gospel of Matthew*, 207.

28. Caragounis, *Peter and the Rock*, 15.

29. Compare Caragounis, *Peter and the Rock*, 89.

30. Carson, "Matthew," 367; Hagner, *Matthew 14–28*, 470; Mitch and Sri, *Gospel of Matthew*, 207.

31. Ratzinger, *Called to Communion*, 60.

32. Caragounis, *Peter and the Rock*, 30.

33. Caragounis, *Peter and the Rock*, 29–30.

This hypothetical double use of *kepha* would in any case have been communicated far more easily in Greek if Matthew were to have used either *petros* or *petra* twice. And this would have been possible if *petros* and *petra* really do mean the same thing! Carson writes: "The Greek makes the distinction between *petros* and *petra* simply because it is trying to preserve the [name/noun] pun, and in Greek the feminine *petra* could not very well serve as a masculine name."[34] *Petros* had to be used for the name and *petra* for the common noun. But this is a *non sequitur* if *petros* and *petra* are synonymous, as Carson himself admits. Nothing stops Matthew from writing: "You are *Petros* and on this *petros*." Matthew also could have written: "You are *petros*/the *petra* and on you." Any one of these possibilities would have made it amply clear that Jesus was referring to Simon, and yet none of them is found in Matthew's Gospel. He has instead: "You are *Petros* and on this *petra*." This more strongly suggests that Matthew did not understand Jesus to be referring to Simon in both cases.

As Garland appreciates, the only obvious reason for Matthew to use two different terms that otherwise mean the same thing in such close succession would be to make clear a difference of referent.[35] There would be no need, for example, to engage in stylistic variation. Matthew does not shy away from using *petra* twice in close succession at 7:24–25 and *petrōdē* twice at 13:5, 20. He is not one to use a variety of synonymous terms unnecessarily. Moreover, the use of one and the same term in both cases would have made the identity of Simon as the referent of both words nearly entirely unambiguous. There was thus a very clear and straightforward way for Matthew to say what the commentators think he must be saying: using the same word twice. He therefore must have used two different terms precisely in order to make clear that Jesus is not actually referring to Simon in both cases. The assumption that *petros* is a common noun applied to Simon and that it is synonymous with *petra* consequently leads to the conclusion that Matthew likely did not think Jesus to be referring to Simon as the rock on which the church is built.

Alternatively, assume that *petros* and *petra* are common nouns that do not mean the same thing. *Petros* is used twice in the LXX to refer to loose rocks or stones that one can pick up in the hands and throw (2 Macc 1:16, 4:41). A *petros* is thus a "detached stone."[36] It is not used in the New Testament at all except as referring to Simon Peter. *Petrōdē* is an adjective that comes from the noun *petros* and is used to describe "rocky ground" (Matt

---

34. Carson, "Matthew," 368.

35. Garland, *Reading Matthew*, 173; cf. Caragounis, *Peter and the Rock*, 90.

36. Gundry, *Matthew*, 334.

13:5, 20). *Petra* is used to refer to bedrock. Jesus describes his teachings using the analogy of a *petra* on which one can build a house that will withstand all storms (7:24–25). There is therefore even less reason to suppose that Simon would be the referent of both *petros* and *petra* in this case. Jesus would be calling Simon something like a rock taken from the bedrock. Or perhaps he would be calling Simon something made of the same stuff as the bedrock. The fact that Jesus already calls his own teachings a *petra* on which one can build (*oikodomeō*) a house would sooner suggest that these teachings or even Jesus himself is the *petra* on which the church is built. Simon is then called *petros* because he appreciates the truth that Jesus is the Messiah of God.[37]

These arguments show that there is no compelling grammatical reason why Simon should be the referent of both *petros* and *petra*. The assumption that *petros* is applied to Simon as a proper name yields the conclusion that he lives up to the significance of this name in virtue of his confession, but this does not mean that he is being called "the rock" any more than a baby girl named "Philippa" by her parents is being called a lover of horses. This only raises the question as to what his name means and how he fulfills its significance. Jesus could be calling Simon *Petros* because he is "of (the) *petra*" in virtue of his recognition of Jesus as the Messiah. To return to Augustine's reading: *Petros* is named after the *petra* just as the "Christian" is named after Christ. His name functions referentially and adjectivally; it describes him in relation to something else outside of him. Neither does the supposition that *petros* is applied to Simon as a common noun demand that he also be the referent of *petra*. *Petros* and *petra* are either synonymous or not. There would be no reason at all for Matthew to use different words in close succession if they were synonymous except apparently to signal a difference of referent, and there would be still less reason for both terms to refer to Simon if they are not synonymous. The pure grammatical analysis of this text consequently does not favor the interpretation that Simon is the *petra* on which the church is built but rather motivates against it.

Many people will nevertheless not be convinced by the grammatical analysis of the passage. They seem to think it is obvious that the application of *Petros* as a name to Simon means that Jesus is calling him a rock. They also think it is equally obvious that Jesus could only be referring to Simon when he says: "On this rock I will build my church." They therefore explain the use of different terms as follows: Jesus had to use *petra* to refer to a bedrock on which the church would be built, but he also had to use the masculine form *Petros* as a proper name for Simon. This makes it possible for Matthew to

37. Gundry, *Matthew*, 334.

preserve the wordplay that would have been evident in Jesus's hypothetical original Aramaic formulation: "You are *kepha* and on this *kepha*."[38] What then can be said by way of response?

The dogmatic impatience of some commentators with any other reading than this one is not convincing.[39] Carson even writes: "[I]f it were not for Protestant reactions against extremes of Roman Catholic interpretation, it is doubtful whether many would have taken 'rock' to be anything or anyone other than Peter."[40] And France: "It is only Protestant overreaction to the Roman Catholic claim . . . that what is here said of Peter applies also to the later bishops of Rome, that has led some to claim that 'rock' here is not Peter at all but the faith which he has just confessed."[41] But such incredulity is in fact specious. A number of patristic commentators did not at all find it obvious that *petra* necessarily referred to Simon himself. John Chrysostom thought that the "rock" referred to Simon's confession of faith in Jesus as the Messiah:

> "Thou art Peter, and upon this rock will I build my Church"; that is, on the faith of his confession. (*Homilies on the Gospel of St. Matthew* 52.3)

John Cassian likewise implies that the belief confessed by Simon that Jesus is God is the rock on which the church is built:

> "[Y]ou are Peter and upon this rock I will build My Church." Do you see how the saying of Peter is the faith of the Church? He then must of course be outside the Church, who does not hold the faith of the Church. (*On the Incarnation of the Lord* 3.14)

And Augustine thought that it referred to Christ who is the rock on which the church is built and after whom Simon is named *Petros*. This interpretation was mentioned earlier (*Sermons on the New Testament* 26.1–2). Consider also this passage:

> I so explained what the Lord said: "Thou art Peter, and upon this rock I will build my Church," that it be understood as built upon him whom Peter confessed saying: "Thou art the Christ, the Son of the living God," and so Peter, called after this rock, represented the person of the Church which is built upon this rock, and has received "the keys of the kingdom of heaven." For,

38. Blomberg, *Matthew*, 252; Carson, "Matthew," 368.

39. See an example in Turner, *Matthew*, 406–7.

40. Carson, "Matthew," 368.

41. France, *Gospel according to Matthew*, 254.

"Thou art Peter" and not "Thou art the rock" was said to him. But "the rock was Christ" [cf. 1 Cor 10:4], in confessing whom, as also the whole Church confesses, Simon was called Peter. (*Retractations* 20.1)

These patristic figures thus did not share the conviction of modern commentators that Simon himself is obviously the referent of *petra*, but they can hardly be accused of reacting as Protestants to the "extremes of Roman Catholic interpretation"! They lived before the differentiation between Protestantism and Roman Catholicism ever existed. It is therefore not quite so obvious as Carson and France suppose that Simon simply must be the referent of *petra*.

One can also propose that this interpretation seems confused as to what it means to say. Is *petros* as applied to Simon a proper name? He is not being called a rock in that case. He is being called *Petros*, and the significance of this name is debatable. Or is it being applied to Simon as a common noun? He is then being called a *petros*. But there would be no reason for Matthew to use two different words if it is applied as a common noun that is synonymous with *petra*, and there is no reason to suppose both terms refer to Simon if they are not synonymous. Which then is it?

This reading seems to be motivated at heart by the conviction that Jesus simply must be referring to Simon when he says: "on this rock." These authors are sure that Jesus cannot have anyone else in mind when using this phrase, and this forms the basis of the rest of the reading. The meaning of the noun/name *petros* is then determined on the foundational assumption that Simon must be the referent of "this *petra*."[42] Hence also the hypothetical supposition of a double use of *kepha*. And yet that Simon is the referent of *petra* cannot be established on grammatical grounds. This reading must therefore be justified on nongrammatical grounds. But what such grounds are there? Is there any reason at all for thinking that Jesus means to say that he will build his church on Simon? Is this something Matthew's Jesus would say?

Some might suppose that it would be awkward for Jesus to be referring to anyone but Simon in saying "on this rock." Blomberg says this phrase "almost certainly refers to Peter."[43] The use of a noun together with the demonstrative adjective ("this rock") suggests that Jesus is talking about someone other than himself, and the only plausible candidate in context is that he is speaking about Simon. Caragounis likewise maintains that the phrase cannot refer to Jesus, even though he believes it refers to the faith that Simon has

---

42. France, *Gospel according to Matthew*, 254.
43. Blomberg, *Matthew*, 252.

confessed rather than to Simon himself.[44] Garland agrees with him in this.[45] But both positions are founded on an invalid inference. Consider what Jesus says to the Jews when he cleanses the temple: "Destroy this temple and in three days I will raise it up" (John 2:19). The Jews understandably took him to be referring to the temple building itself where they were all located (v. 20), yet John clarifies that Jesus was in fact referring to the "temple" of his body (v. 21). This is something the disciples realized not then and there but only after his resurrection (v. 22). Jesus thus can refer to himself in a figurative, confusing, and counter-contextual way by using a noun paired with a demonstrative adjective ("this temple"), and there is nothing preventing him from doing the same thing in the episode recounted in Matthew's Gospel. Jesus could be saying to Simon: "You are *Petros* = of (the) *petra*, and on this *petra* = on myself I will build my church."

It is thus not impossible that Jesus should have been referring to himself in saying "on this rock." There is admittedly nothing about the words themselves or the immediate context of his speech that suggests this interpretation in any obvious way, but the same thing is true of his saying recorded in John's Gospel: "Destroy this temple." The Evangelist insists that he was referring to himself there (John 2:19, 21). And Matthew even knows about the temple saying (Matt 26:61; 27:40). Jesus can therefore also be referring to himself in Matthew's text. But can any arguments be given for preferring this reading to the alternative?

Here is the true question: whether there are any reasons in Matthew's Gospel for thinking it more plausible or reasonable that Jesus would be building his church on himself rather than on Peter. In fact there are. It is far more consistent with the depiction of Jesus in Matthew's Gospel to suppose him to be saying that he will build the church upon himself, and it is positively inconsistent with the depiction of Simon in Matthew's Gospel to suppose Jesus to be saying that he is the rock on which the church will be built. Making this latter supposition will even have the unfortunate consequence of turning Matthew's Gospel into a polemic against Simon more than anything else. It is therefore better to think that Jesus is referring to himself. This fits best with Matthew's presentation of Jesus and Simon alike. This point can be appreciated as follows.

On the one hand, Matthew depicts Jesus as someone who claims to be uniquely authoritative in all matters theological. His teachings are like a solid bedrock (*petra*) on which one can build one's life and become invulnerable to every passing storm (7:24–25). He teaches with an authority that

44. Caragounis, *Peter and the Rock*, 88–89.

45. Garland, *Reading Matthew*, 174.

even the scribes and Pharisees do not claim for themselves (vv. 28–29). As Blomberg comments: "Strikingly, Jesus quotes Scripture in his sermon only to reinterpret it, he cites no human authorities or tradition, and he speaks with directness and confidence that he himself is bringing God's message for a new era in human history."[46] Jesus claims that he alone knows God the Father and is capable of revealing him to others (11:27). He calls all people to take on the light and easy "yoke" of his teachings (vv. 28–30). He calls himself the "lord of the sabbath" (12:8). He calls himself the "stone" (*lithos*) that builders rejected which eventually became the cornerstone of the house (21:42). He claims that he alone is teacher and that all his disciples are brothers and equally his students (23:8, 10). Finally, he receives all authority in heaven and on earth from the Father and commissions all his eleven disciples specifically to go into the world and to teach others the very things that he has taught them (28:18–20). There is consequently nothing at all about Jesus as Matthew depicts him which predicts or anticipates the notion that he would establish Simon as the *petra* on which his church would be built. What in Jesus's words would foreshadow or even allow for it? Indeed, why would Matthew's Jesus ever consider such a thing at all? The most important teachings of Jesus are always ultimately about himself; Jesus always points to himself. It is thus more consistent with Jesus's conception of himself in the Gospel according to Matthew to suppose that he would say that he will build the church upon himself.

But how could Jesus build the church upon himself? Carson comments: "In this passage Jesus is the builder of the church and it would be a strange mixture of metaphors that also sees him within the same clauses as its foundation."[47] Yet the matter is not so mysterious as it may seem. Jesus says: "Come to me, all you who are weary and burdened, and I will give you rest" (11:28). And he commissions his disciples after his resurrection: "Go then and make disciples of all nations, . . . teaching them to obey everything that I have commanded you" (28:19–20). This is therefore how Jesus builds the church upon himself as its foundation: by making others into his disciples and students of his teachings.

On the other hand, Matthew's depiction of Simon in the Gospel is almost entirely negative. He apparently cannot do anything right. He never seems to be on the same wavelength as Jesus. It is true that Matthew lists "Simon, the one called Peter" as "first" in Jesus's list of the twelve apostles (Matt 10:2). But this could mean no more than that he was the first one called by Jesus on that occasion to be given authority over unclean spirits and illnesses

46. Blomberg, *Matthew*, 134–35.
47. Carson, "Matthew," 368.

(10:1). There is nothing about the adjective "first" that demands that Simon somehow occupied a uniquely privileged rank among the apostles. The episode at 16:17–19 is effectively the only instance in which something positive is said about Simon at all, and the depiction of Simon becomes even more negative after it. Simon falls into the lake because of his lack of faith in Jesus (14:28–31). He does not understand Jesus's "parable" about what does and does not make unclean (15:8). He brazenly and inappropriately rebukes Jesus when he teaches that he will be rejected and crucified (16:22). Jesus responds by calling him "satan" and telling him that he does not have his mind on the things of God (16:23). Simon speaks nonsense during the transfiguration and is interrupted by the divine voice (17:4–5). He asks a question that makes him seem unwilling to forgive (18:21). He expresses a concern for the material compensations to be expected for following Jesus (19:27). He arrogantly claims perfect allegiance to Jesus only to be told right after that he will in fact deny him three times (26:33–35). He proves unable to remain in prayer with Jesus for even an hour (26:40). Worst of all, the very last mention of Simon by name is the reference to his curse, triple denial of Jesus, and bitter weeping (26:75). He is not specifically mentioned again after this point in the Gospel according to Matthew.

Consider therefore how Matthew depicts both Jesus and Simon. Jesus understands himself as a unique authority, whereas Simon is a blundering disciple last mentioned by name at his apostasy in Jesus's hour of trial. Is there any reason at all then to suppose that Matthew's Jesus would be installing Simon as the rock on which the church will be built? Nothing about Jesus's explicit self-conception as related by Matthew anticipates or motivates such a reading. Jesus never points to someone else; he only ever points to himself. He only ever gives the impression of considering himself to be the rock on which he would build his own church, and he is the only character in Matthew's Gospel worthy of the title. Likewise, nothing in Matthew's depiction of Simon gives any impression that Matthew thought of him as the rock on which the church is built. He seemingly never acts in the way one would expect of the rock of the church. Indeed, there is nothing about his confession of Jesus as the Messiah which would motivate Jesus to name him the rock on which the church is built, since the other disciples already made this same confession apart from him when they were in the boat during the storm (14:33). It thus seems more coherent with Matthew's depiction of things to say that Jesus rather than Simon is the rock on which the church is built. This is the conclusion motivated by Matthew's text itself rather than by irrelevant dogmatic precommitments.

The negative depiction of Simon in Matthew's Gospel cannot be ignored. Caragounis summarizes the point: "Peter is presented by Matthew as confused, cowardly, without understanding, disliking suffering, giving with a view to future gain, impetuous, impulsive and unstable, stingy in forgiving, overestimating his ability, and denying his Master miserably."[48] And Garland: "The fifteen incidents in the Gospel that specifically involve him portray him as rash, confused, desirous of reward, over-confident, faltering, and cowardly—in other words, he represents a normal disciple."[49] At least one scholar even goes so far as to say that Matthew thinks of Simon as an apostate and a false disciple.[50] This can admittedly seem an extreme opinion, and it is not the perspective being adopted here. Simon seems clearly to be dear to Jesus and to other Christians in the whole of the New Testament. France even writes that it is "a matter of historic fact that Peter was the acknowledged leader of the group of disciples, and of the developing church in its early years."[51] But this sentence is only acceptable in a certain sense. Sometimes one person out of a group of friends is more prominent than the rest as a result of his or her personality. Simon may have been such a person in comparison to the other apostles. He is most notable among the apostles in virtue of his personality. But this is hardly grounds for saying that Simon occupies a special place in any official "hierarchy."

There is also the following point to be made on this score. Leave to the side the fact that Matthew's audience may not have had access to everything said about Simon elsewhere in the New Testament. It is one thing for Simon to be dear to Jesus, and it is another altogether for him to be the *petra* on which the church is built. One had might as well argue that John is greater than Simon because he alone is described as "the disciple whom Jesus loved." The personal connection between Jesus and any one of his disciples does not necessarily translate into their being situated in a privileged position within a hierarchy. Blomberg even writes that "Matthew paints a consistently negative or at least ambiguous portrait of Peter, which may make it more probable that he was trying to temper an already overexalted view of that apostle."[52] One must therefore consider the matter more carefully.

Suppose that Matthew thought Simon was the rock on which Jesus said he would build the church. Why then does the depiction of Simon become increasingly negative as time goes on? Why would the last mention of Simon by name in the Gospel be his curse, triple denial, and bitter

48. Caragounis, *Peter and the Rock*, 99.

49. Garland, *Reading Matthew*, 174.

50. See Gundry, *Peter*.

51. France, *Gospel according to Matthew*, 255.

52. Blomberg, *Matthew*, 255.

weeping? Why is there no narrative of Simon's restoration to Jesus after his denial as in the other Gospels (John 21:15–20; cf. Mark 16:7)? Why does Simon disappear into the crowd of the "eleven" by the time Jesus gives them the "great commission" on the mountain after his resurrection (28:16–20)? What would it mean for Matthew to write like this about a person who had received the lofty title of "rock" on which Jesus would build the church? Would it make any sense to write a story about the disciple chosen by Jesus to be the foundation of the church and to end the narrative in this way?

Two possibilities suggest themselves. On the one hand, Matthew could have thought that Simon was indeed named the rock on which the church would be built but then lost this privilege and honor after his apostasy. This proposal (rather implausibly and regrettably?) turns Matthew's Gospel into an anti-Petrine polemic; Matthew becomes an opponent of Simon and of the idea of his primacy among all the apostles. Leo the Great would write: "Anyone who thinks that the primacy should be denied to Peter cannot in any way lessen the Apostle's dignity; inflated with the wind of his own pride, he buries himself in hell" (*Letters* 10). One might think that this insistence on the primacy of Peter would then turn into an accusation against the evangelist Matthew himself. On the other hand, one may say alternatively that Matthew never understood Simon to be the *petra* on which the church could be built in the first place. This *petra* is instead Jesus. This also explains why Matthew uses two different words at 16:18a–b. It means that Simon is for Matthew at best a representation of the weakness and folly of every Christian.[53] He is a parable for showing how every Christian must cling to Christ as the rock on which he or she is built up into the church.

Caragounis agrees that Simon is not the *petra*. He argues instead that the *petra* on which the church is built is the fact which Simon confesses: that Jesus is the Messiah.[54] This reading agrees with Chrysostom as noted above (*Homilies on the Gospel of St. Matthew* 52.3). The proposal being made here is that Jesus himself is the rock. These readings are perhaps not radically different, but it seems better to say that Jesus is the rock rather than the sentence that Peter confesses. The sentence cannot do the founding work if Jesus is not actually the Messiah. The sentence must be true if it is going to serve as a foundation for the messianic community. Yet a sentence is not true in itself but rather because of what it refers to. Jesus himself is what makes the sentence about him true. It would then seem to follow that Jesus himself is in a truer and more ultimate sense the rock on which the church will be built.

---

53. Gundry, *Matthew*, 334.
54. Caragounis, *Peter and the Rock*, 113.

Recall then that a significant proportion of scholars think it is simply obvious that Jesus must have been referring to Simon when saying "on this rock." They assume that this is the only reasonable or obvious way to read the text and have little to no patience for the alternative view. Yet the argument of the preceding paragraphs has tried to show that their confidence in this particular reading is exaggerated. There is nothing grammatically necessary about it. One can scarcely make sense of the fact that Matthew apparently unnecessarily uses two different words (*petros* and *petra*) if he thought Jesus was referring to Simon in both cases. He could more easily have got the point across by writing *petros* or *petra* twice. This is especially obvious if *petros* and *petra* mean the same thing, as so many commentators say. It is furthermore not at all impossible for Jesus to have been referring to himself in saying "on this rock." He does this in John's Gospel when he says: "Destroy this temple" (John 2:19, 21). Matthew also knew of this saying (Matt 26:61; 27:40). It was thus possible for Jesus to speak this way irrespective of how contextually confusing it may have been. And it can likewise now be appreciated that the very idea that Simon should be the rock on which the church is built is inconsonant with Matthew's depiction of both Jesus and Simon. Jesus in Matthew's Gospel claims unique and ultimate theological authority for himself alone; he is in a way the ultimate subject matter of all his most important teachings. Simon in Matthew's Gospel is almost never depicted especially positively. The final mention of him by name is his curse, triple denial of Jesus, and bitter weeping. Matthew doesn't say anything about Simon in particular after that. Nothing about Jesus's self-conception in Matthew predicts or motivates ascribing to Simon the role of the "rock" on which he would build the church, and nothing in Matthew's depiction of Simon in the Gospel indicates that the evangelist thought of Simon in this way. A strong case can therefore be made that reading Jesus as referring to Simon in saying "on this rock" makes little sense in light of the rest of Matthew's Gospel. It is better to think of Jesus as referring to himself. Simon is called *Petros* because he recognizes Jesus, who is the *petra* on which the church will be built. And this is consistent with Jesus's denial of "hierarchy" among his disciples.

THE GATES OF HADES

Simon is called *Petros* because, in virtue of his confession of Jesus as Messiah, he is "of (the) *petra*." He is named "Peter" after the *petra* of Jesus whom he confesses just as Christians are called "Christians" after the Christ in whom they believe. Jesus thus tells him: "You are *Petros* = of (the) *petra*, and on this *petra* = on myself I will build my church [*ekklēsian*], and the gates of Hades will not prevail against it [*autēs*]." But a further question arises at this point. What is the "it" (*autēs*) against which the gates of Hades will not prevail?

The apparently most natural reading for many is that "it" refers to the church. This is because "church" is the nearest relevant noun to which "it" could refer. But it is also possible in principle for the pronoun to refer to the feminine noun *petra*. Such a reading does indeed have some historical precedent. For example, Origen speaks of "Peter, against whom the gates of hell do not prevail" (*On First Principles* 3, 2, 5). Veselin Kesich notes this and a few other passages in which Origen makes a similar remark.[55] This interpretation admittedly identifies Simon with the *petra*, but it is remarkable for implying that the *autēs* against which the gates of Hades will not prevail is the *petra* rather than the *ekklēsian*. Suppose then that one identifies the *petra* with Jesus. It is therefore possible to say that the gates of Hades will not prevail against the *petra* which refers to Jesus. But are there any reasons for reading the text this way? Indeed there are.

This would make sense in the light of the New Testament's way of speaking about things. Jesus is twice put in connection with Hades as its conqueror in the Bible. First, Simon refers to Jesus in his Pentecost sermon as the Holy One whom God would not abandon to Hades (Acts 2:27, 31). Second, Jesus himself in Revelation says the following: "I was dead, yet behold, I am alive unto the ages of ages, and I have the keys of death and of Hades" (Rev 1:18). Jesus is thus the conqueror of Hades because he rose from the dead. Yet Simon and the church are never said to have conquered Hades in Scripture; they are never even mentioned in connection with Hades in the whole of the New Testament. This was apparently not a common way of speaking in the apostolic generation of Christians. It therefore seems better to think that the "it" against which the gates of Hades will not prevail is Jesus the *petra*. This is a sentence about Jesus's imminent death and resurrection as a conquest of Hades. And it is not coincidental that Matthew will go on to mention in the verses that immediately follow that Jesus begins to teach about his impending death and resurrection (Matt 16:21).

A case can therefore be made that the "it" (*autēs*) against which the gates of Hades will not prevail is Jesus the *petra* who will die and rise again. He will conquer Hades and thus prevail over its gates by his resurrection. This is also how the church can be built on him as its foundation.

55. Kesich, "Peter's Primacy," 65.

THE KEYS OF THE KINGDOM

Jesus and not Simon is the *petra* on which the church is built and against which the gates of Hades will not prevail because he will be raised from the dead. Recognizing this point makes it possible to interpret the subsequent statement which Jesus makes to Simon: "I will give you the keys of the kingdom of heaven, and whatever you bind on earth will have been bound in heaven, and whatever you loose on earth will have been loosed in heaven" (Matt 16:19).

Many interpreters think that the mention of "the keys of the kingdom of heaven" here hearkens back in some way or other to Isaiah's mention of "the key of the house of David" (Isa 22:22).[56] This Old Testament passage refers to the replacement of Shebna by Eliakim as the "master of the household" or "chief steward" in the kingdom of Judah (v. 15). He is a kind of "second-in-command" after the king himself. Eliakim will even use the "key of the house of David" in such a way that "he shall open, and no one shall shut; he shall shut, and no one shall open" (v. 22). These commentators therefore propose that something similar is happening to Simon as well. "I will give you the keys of the kingdom of heaven" means: "I will make you second-in-command in my kingdom."[57] "Whatever you bind on earth will have been bound in heaven" means something like: "You will make decisions about things that no one will be permitted to challenge or question."

This is a reading of the passage that is both "traditionalist" and "hierarchical." It is "traditionalist" because it supposes that Simon will have the authority to make binding and definitive decisions about matters of practice and faith in the church that must always be obeyed by all persons. It understands the "binding" and "loosing" that Simon will be doing to be analogous to that authority which the Pharisees presumed for themselves and for the traditions of the elders. It is also "hierarchical" because it presumes that this authority is given to Simon and not also to all other disciples. Neal Judisch thus recounts his recognizing this interpretation of the passage as a step in coming to his "initial, surprised discovery that 'papism' was perhaps not solely a deliverance of extrabiblical 'tradition,' designed to clothe what would otherwise have been a naked grab for earthly power."[58] He sees here evidence that Jesus granted Simon with "the symbols of administrative and disciplinary authority over David's house . . . the keys

---

56. Blomberg, *Matthew*, 254; Carson, "Matthew," 370; Evans, *Matthew*, 314; Mitch and Sri, *Gospel of Matthew*, 209; Talbert, *Matthew*, 196; Turner, *Matthew*, 407.

57. See Mitch and Sri, *Gospel of Matthew*, 209.

58. Judisch, "Of Towers and Tongues," 120.

of the kingdom and the power to bind and loose with finality."[59] What then can be said by way of response?

The first point to make is that arguments have already been offered from Matthew's Gospel itself against attributing to Jesus either the idea of "traditionalism" or that of "hierarchy." Jesus clearly rejects "traditionalism" in his anti-Pharisaical polemics. He believes that every human tradition must always be measured against the commandments of God (Matt 15:9). This implies that no merely human figures possess "finality." Even Simon himself then could not be beyond all questioning in what he says. It also implies that the commandment of God is always separable and distinct from any human tradition. Human traditions are at best testimonies and acts of witnessing to the words of God rather than being the means by which God himself speaks. Thus God and Jesus alone possess original, infallible, and irreversible theological authority, while all others' authority is only derivative and fallibly and in principle reversibly exercised. This means that Simon is not guaranteed to be correct in what he binds or looses unless he manages to communicate Jesus's teachings. Jesus likewise clearly rejects "hierarchy" when he tells his disciples: "You are not to be called 'rabbi,' for you all have one teacher while you are all brothers. . . Neither are you to be called instructors, for the Messiah alone is your instructor" (23:8, 10). What sense is there in calling Simon a "second-in-command" only later to say that all disciples of Jesus are brothers and equally students of one and the same Messiah? Either they are all equally brothers and students or else Simon is a "second-in-command," but both cannot be true; not everyone would be a "second-in-command" and thus not all would be equal. This reading is therefore inconsistent with Jesus's rejection of "traditionalism" and "hierarchy" elsewhere in this very Gospel of Matthew.

The second point to make about this reading is that its interpretation of the connection between the Matthean passage and the prophecy from Isaiah is contentious and far from obvious. It assumes that one and the same thing must be happening in Matthew as in Isaiah. But Matthew often refers to "images" from the Old Testament by which to make sense of what is happening in Jesus. He even says that the New Testament event "fulfills" the image from the Old. Yet this does not mean that one and the same thing is happening in Jesus's time that was happening in the Old Testament passage as well; the two events can actually be radically different with only a superficial resemblance. The prime example is the "prophecy": "Out of Egypt I called my Son" (Hos 11:1; Matt 2:15). Hosea refers to the Exodus while Matthew refers to Jesus's return from Egypt to Palestine in his childhood. The

---

59. Judisch, "Of Towers and Tongues," 119.

two events have hardly any resemblance. The Jews escaped physical slavery in Egypt; their escape was preceded by a series of plagues; they commemorated this event every year through the slaughtering of a lamb. Jesus's family were refugees in Egypt fleeing persecution in Palestine; their escape was preceded only by the death of Herod far away; this event is only mentioned once and without much circumstance in all of the New Testament. Two very different things were thus happening. One could not have predicted Jesus's flight from Egypt on the basis of the Hosea text, and yet Matthew says that what happens in Jesus "fulfills" what happened to Israel. One could say that Matthew understands God to have "foreshadowed" the flight from Egypt by means of the Hosean reference to the Exodus in a way that could only become evident after the flight from Egypt itself had actually occurred. The Old Testament passage therefore can provide an image that is reflected in what happens to Jesus without one and the same thing happening in both cases.

The epistle to the Hebrews calls the Law a "shadow" of the good things to come (Heb 10:1). This is a very useful category for thinking of the relationship between Old and New Testaments. A "shadow" only bears a resemblance to the shape of the thing of which it is the shadow when seen from a particular angle; the shadow can appear very different from the thing itself if seen from some other perspective. The shadow of one's fingers may look like a rabbit or a man with a hat while one's fingers themselves look nothing like that. It is even physically and perceptually impossible for a shadow to resemble the shape of the thing of which it is the shadow from any other angle except precisely that of the light source.

This insight should therefore be applied to the relationship between the Old and New Testaments as well. The things in the Old Testament are shadows or even "foreshadows" of the things in the New. They have the "shape" of the events described in the New Testament—but only when perceived from a certain angle. One must also note that the evangelists and New Testament authors did not interpret what Jesus did in light of some prior understanding of the Old Testament. It is rather that they began to read the Old Testament in light of what they had independently seen in Jesus. And the Old Testament text can be seen as a "shadow" or "foreshadow" of the thing that took place in Jesus only if what took place in Jesus can be understood on its own terms. Only so would one know what would or would not count as its "shadow"; one cannot tell what counts as "foreshadowing" until the whole narrative has been read. Thus, it is not that Matthew thought Jesus had to go to Egypt as a child and return in order to "fulfill" the text from Hosea, but rather that Matthew's knowledge of this event in Jesus's life made it possible for him to see its "foreshadow" in Hosea's lines in the first place.[60] He is not inventing Jesus's history in line with a prior conception of what the Old Testament predicts about it, but rather assigning a new meaning to the Old Testament in light of what he independently knows to be the story of Jesus. The independent event in Jesus's history is like a light being shone which then casts shadows into the Old Testament.

There is consequently no need at all for the Old and New Testament events to share the same logic or meaning. What happens to Jesus need not be exactly what happened in the case of the Old Testament "shadow" to which an evangelist might make reference. One might also put the matter a bit more forcefully and say that it is positively fallacious to propose that an event described in the New Testament must be interpreted according to the logic and meaning of the Old Testament event to which it is purportedly related. And this also militates against the idea that Jesus is making Simon a "second-in-command" within his kingdom just as God was doing by replacing Shebna with Eliakim.

The third point to make in connection with these passages is that there is not obviously more than a superficial relation between them. Matthew himself does not here propose any explicit connection to the Isaiah prophecy as he does in other places (e.g., Matt 2:5–6, 14–15, 17–18, 23). He does not say here as elsewhere that this conversation between Jesus and Simon took place to "fulfill" something from the Old Testament. Furthermore, there are a number of differences in wording. Isaiah mentions a "key" while Matthew speaks of "keys"; the prophet speaks of the key "of the house of David" while Jesus references the keys "of the kingdom of heaven"; Isaiah speaks about opening and shutting in a way that no one can undo, whereas Matthew references binding and loosing on earth in accordance with the condition of heaven. Why then think that there is anything more than a superficial resemblance between these passages? Why think that the one passage simply must be read in the light of the other to which it makes no explicit reference? Matthew's Jesus could have remained much closer to the original phrasing of the text from Isaiah if he wished to make clear that he is establishing Simon as a kind of "chief steward" of the church just as God was doing with Eliakim. But what one actually finds in the Matthean text are mere impressions or suggestions of a resemblance which do not obviously demand any one particular interpretation.

Does this necessarily mean that there is no connection between the passages at all? No. It is just that the connection could be something other than the idea that Simon is being set up as a "second-in-command" in Jesus's

60. Evans, *Matthew*, 63.

church. It could be instead that Simon is being given something by which he will exercise a definitive heavenly authority in the church and in the whole world, even without himself being a part of any "hierarchy." The exact meaning of this alternative will be clarified in the discussion that follows.

There is consequently not very much to be said in favor of the notion that Jesus is establishing Simon as a "second-in-command" within the messianic community of his church. This reading is incompatible with Jesus's rejection of "traditionalism" and "hierarchy" elsewhere in Matthew's Gospel. It likewise fallaciously assumes a particular relationship between the Matthean text and the Old Testament which is far from obvious and not particularly supported by the Matthean text itself. Finally, the resemblances between Matt 16:19 and Isa 22:15–25 are few and superficial and thus open to multiple interpretations. The question then becomes whether there is an alternative reading to be given that is consistent with Jesus's rejection of both "traditionalism" and "hierarchy." In fact there is. "I will give you the keys of the kingdom of heaven" can be taken as meaning something along the following lines: "I will give you something by which you will open up and shut the kingdom of heaven to people."

The earlier reading assumed that "keys" were a symbol of authority. This is how Hagner reads the passage.[61] Garland agrees with him: "To give the keys to someone meant to confer authority on that person (Rev 1:18; 3:7). The keys are an image for stewardship of God's affairs on earth."[62] Jesus was certainly establishing Simon as an authority within the church by giving him the "keys." But why should "keys" mean "authority" *simpliciter*? There is another way to understand the metaphor readily available. Consider that keys are not just symbols of authority. Keys are things one uses to open and shut doors. They are not symbols of a general and undefined authority but rather tools by which one exercises a very particular authority. Moreover, all keys necessarily have a fixed size and shape, and this size and shape of a key determines what it can and cannot open. The key to one's house cannot open the doors of another's car, just as the key to a safe will not open a shed. Keys are always keys for a particular end; they always open particular things. This must therefore be kept in mind when Jesus says that he will give Simon the "keys of the kingdom of heaven." He is not saying that he will be making Simon a "second-in-command" over the church. He is rather saying that he will hand over to Simon something by which the kingdom of heaven will be opened up and shut to others.

61. Hagner, *Matthew 14–28*, 472.

62. Garland, *Reading Matthew*, 175.

What are the "keys" by which Simon will open and shut the kingdom of heaven to others? The obvious answer to give from Matthew's Gospel is: the teachings of Jesus. That one's sins are forgiven by God; that one is to think of God, the source of one's life and of all things, as one's Father; that one should love God with all one's being; that one should believe in Jesus; that one should love one's neighbor as oneself; that one should pray in all circumstances with the childlike confidence of receiving what one asks for—these teachings are what open the kingdom of heaven to a person if they are accepted or else close it if they are rejected. They are the "words of the kingdom" (13:19). They are what make it possible for one to enter into the "kingdom of heaven." This latter phrase refers to that condition of things in which God's will is done on earth as it is in heaven (Matt 6:10). It refers to "the presence and reign of God."[63] The kingdom of heaven is a state of harmony between Creator and created order; it is a matter of being reconciled to God as the source of one's life and being in the intimacy of one's own conscience which further makes it possible to live differently in the world. This is why Jesus will say: "Unless your righteousness exceeds that of the scribes and of the Pharisees, you will never enter into the kingdom of heaven" (5:20). He says this because the teachings of the scribes and Pharisees are not enough. One needs the teachings of Jesus. It is not necessarily that the Pharisees' teachings are insufficiently exigent or anything of the sort, but rather that their teachings actually "shut up the kingdom of heaven before people" and turn their converts into "children of Gehenna" (23:13, 15). They do not make God present or show his reign; a person is not brought into harmony with God's will by following the teachings of the scribes and the Pharisees; they do not give one the freedom of life that comes with the conviction that God is one's Father. One must rather be taught by Jesus who has the audacity to say: "You have heard that it was said . . . But I say to you . . ." (5:21–22, 27–28, 31–32, 33–34, 38–39). Only Jesus's teachings can serve as a solid bedrock (*petra*) on which one can build one's life in such a way as to be able to withstand any storm (7:24–25). He alone knows God the Father and can reveal him to others (11:27). But the goal of theological authority is precisely to propose what others must (not) do in order to enter into or remain in friendship with God. This condition of being in friendship with God is precisely the kingdom of heaven. The teachings of Jesus are therefore the "tools" by which theological authority is exercised. Simon will be receiving "keys" in the sense of receiving Jesus's teachings by which the kingdom of heaven will be opened and shut to others in a definitive way that cannot be undone by anyone else.

---

63. Evans, *Matthew*, 94.

This sort of interpretation is not without precedent in history. It was already noted above how John Cassian implies that the rock on which the church is built is the faith in the divinity of Jesus that Simon confessed. He then goes on to say:

> This faith deserved heaven: this faith received the keys of the heavenly kingdom. See what awaits you. You cannot enter the gate to which this key belongs, if you have denied the faith of this key. . . The perfect faith of the Apostle somehow is given the power of Deity, that what it should bind or loose on earth, might be bound or loosed in heaven. For you then, who come against the Apostle's faith, as you see that already you are bound on earth, it only remains that you should know that you are bound also in heaven. (*On the Incarnation of the Lord* 3.14)

He is thus clear that the "keys" that open up the kingdom of heaven are the faith that Simon confesses in Jesus as the Son of God. The kingdom is opened to the one who accepts this faith and closed to the one who rejects it. Huldrych Zwingli too would later argue in various ways that the "keys" are really the gospel message. When it is preached, this message opens up the kingdom of heaven to those who receive it in faith and are regenerated by the Holy Spirit.[64] But these are both different and less general ways of saying the very thing being proposed here. The "keys" of the kingdom of heaven are Jesus's teachings. These teachings are about him and his Father (Matt 11:27). They are the "gospel of the kingdom" (4:23). It is his teachings that open and shut the kingdom of heaven to those who accept or reject them.

The "keys" then are Jesus's teachings. But when are the "keys" to be given to Simon? Jesus used the future tense: "I will give you" (*dōsō soi*). Zwingli argues that this presumably means that they were not given then when he was speaking. They must have been given at a later point in time.[65] The most obvious answer to be drawn from Matthew's Gospel as to when this happened is that the keys were given at the "great commission." Jesus gathers his eleven disciples to him on a mountain after his resurrection and tells them these words: "All authority has been given to me in heaven and on earth. Therefore, go and make disciples of all nations, baptizing them in the name of the Father and of the Son and of the Holy Spirit, teaching them to observe all the things I have commanded you" (28:18–20). Here is therefore the moment when the "keys" are given to Simon: when he is presented with the responsibility and task of going into all the world and opening up and closing the kingdom of heaven to others after the resurrection of Jesus.

64. Zwingli, *Commentary on True and False Religion*, 157–76.
65. Zwingli, *Commentary on True and False Religion*, 162–63.

There are three important things to be noted about this giving of the keys. First, this commission is given to all the eleven disciples (28:16) and not just to Simon. There is even a sense in which this commission is valid and applicable to all Christians. Every Christian in some way or another enjoys both the ability and the responsibility of sharing the teachings of Jesus with others and "making disciples of all nations." The keys are therefore not given only to Simon. He is not distinguished from others in any qualitative way within the messianic community. As Carson writes: "[N]otions of hierarchy or sacerdotalism are simply irrelevant to the text."[66]

Second, Simon together with the other apostles are not commissioned to do anything other than to make disciples of all the nations by sharing the teachings of Jesus. Most importantly of all, they are not given an authority to pass on their own interpretations of things and to impose their own opinions and judgments on others; Jesus never says any such thing to them. Their only authorization is that of teaching others to obey everything that Jesus first commanded them. They are to relate and bear witness to Jesus's teachings and to what God has done in him.

Third, this commission takes place after the resurrection. It is therefore coincident with the order of Jesus's saying to Simon. Jesus says that he will build his church on the rock of himself against which the gates of Hades will not prevail, then he will give Simon the keys of the kingdom of heaven. This is also how things happened in Matthew's narrative. Jesus first dies and rises from the dead; this is his conquest of the gates of Hades. He then commissions Simon together with the other disciples to go into the world and to make disciples of all nations by relating his teachings; this is the handing over of the keys. This is therefore how Jesus builds the church on the rock that he is: he dies and rises from the dead and makes all the nations his disciples and followers of his teachings through the commission of the apostles.

These three points are consonant with the rejection of "traditionalism" and "hierarchy." Only God and Jesus exercise theological authority in an original, infallible, and irreversible way. All other persons—even the apostles themselves—only exercise theological authority in a derivative, fallible, and in principle reversible way. They are authorized to relate and bear witness to the teachings of Jesus and the works of God in him. These are their "tools." Their exercises of theological authority are legitimate when they propose something to be done or believed for the sake of friendship with God because it is Jesus's teaching, and all such exercises are likewise successful when they manage to pass on something that Jesus actually did

66. Carson, "Matthew," 374.

teach. Their attempts become illegitimate or unsuccessful if either of these conditions should not be met. Thus Carson once more: "It appears, then, that the text [of Matt 16:18–19] is not interested in whether Peter's (or the church's) decisions are infallible."[67]

It is therefore possible to interpret the image of the "keys of the kingdom of heaven" in a way that does not imply the notions of "traditionalism" or "hierarchy." "I will give you the keys" does not mean: "I will make you a chief steward over the church." It means rather: "I will give you keys by which you will open up and close the kingdom of heaven to others." Now Simon is certainly being granted an authority in being handed the "keys," so that in this there is an analogy with Eliakim. But the "keys" given to Simon are not simply a figurative reference to authority in general. They are rather specific tools by which Simon will accomplish the task of opening and shutting the kingdom of heaven to people. These "keys" are the teachings of Jesus. They are given to Simon and indeed to all the eleven disciples after Jesus's resurrection at the "great commission" (28:18–20). Hence Simon is given authority in the sense of being given Jesus's teachings and told to propagate them. But it also becomes clear from this that he and all the apostles of Jesus have no other theological authority than that of passing on the teachings they received from Jesus to others and thus making disciples of all nations.

This interpretation is compatible with Jesus's rejection of "traditionalism" and "hierarchy" elsewhere in Matthew's Gospel. It does not posit excessively and unjustifiably specific connections between the Matthean text and the questionable parallel in Isaiah's prophecy to Shebna. This reading is also compatible with admitting at least the following connection between the passages: Simon like Eliakim receives "keys" that grant him a certain authority. These "keys" in Simon's case are the teachings of Jesus by which he will open and shut the kingdom of heaven to people in a definitive way that cannot be undone by anyone else. His opening and shutting cannot be undone by anyone else (similarly to Eliakim) because Jesus's teachings alone can open and shut the kingdom of heaven to anyone. Friendship with God cannot be taken away from anyone who embraces these teachings. It is thus the keys themselves rather than any position within a purported "hierarchy" which make for the irreversibility of Simon's action. But this reading is also consistent with the thesis of the present essay that God and Jesus alone exercise theological authority in an original, infallible, and irreversible way. Simon's action is only irreversible when he succeeds in relating and bearing witness to the teachings of Jesus and the works of God in him.

67. Carson, "Matthew," 374.

BINDING AND LOOSING

The final thing that Jesus says to Simon on this occasion is the following: "Whatever you bind on earth will have been bound in heaven, and whatever you loose on earth will have been loosed in heaven" (16:19). This too must be interpreted.

Many commentators make note of the use of "rabbinic" or "Pharisaical" language here. "Binding" and "loosing" in the mouths of these figures meant exercising the authority to make binding and definitive judgments about the interpretation of the Law.[68] The Pharisees claimed for themselves the right to forbid, permit, or obligate certain practices or ideas and even to include or exclude others from the community.[69] These commentators therefore understand Jesus to be giving Simon the same authority that the Pharisees presumed for themselves.[70] But this reading would once more have Jesus introducing into his own church the same "traditionalism" and "hierarchy" to which he objected in the Pharisees. Jesus would be installing in his own church the sickness that he diagnosed in the Pharisees. This is contrary to what Jesus teaches elsewhere in Matthew's Gospel. Yet there is fortunately another way of reading the text that does not demand conceiving of the church in "traditionalist" or "hierarchical" terms at all.

Jesus says to Simon: "Whatever you bind on earth will have been bound in heaven." This text is also commonly translated: "Whatever you bind on earth will be bound in heaven." The former translation is more literal to the original Greek text, but the second also is common. What is the difference between "will have been" and "will be"?

One might suggest that the difference lies in whether Simon will be guided by God to bind and loose the right things, or else God will subsequently ratify whatever decisions to bind or loose Simon happens to make.[71] It is a difference with respect to whose binding comes first. Either Simon will only bind what will already have been bound in heaven, or else heaven will also bind what Simon himself binds on earth. But the different interpretative options are in fact equally possible no matter how one renders the Greek text. Jesus does not specify the time relative to which the binding on earth is seen in relation to the binding in heaven. One could thus easily say that whatever Simon binds on earth "will be" bound in heaven

---

68. Blomberg, *Matthew*, 254.

69. Singer, *Jewish Encyclopedia*, 215; Mansoor, "Pharisees," 31; Josephus, *War* 1:111, 113.

70. Mitch and Sri, *Gospel of Matthew*, 210.

71. Talbert, *Matthew*, 196–97.

in the sense of already being bound in heaven. Alternatively, one could say that whatever Simon binds on earth "will have been" bound in heaven specifically at the judgment of the last day, because heaven will have followed Simon's lead. This text is therefore equally compatible with either notion, regardless of how the Greek original is translated into English.

Yet it is also possible to propose an entirely different reading. Jesus says to Simon: "I will give you the keys of the kingdom of heaven, and whatever you bind on earth will have been bound in heaven." This does not mean: "You will be providentially guided by God in your decisions to bind or loose." That would just be another appeal to the notion of "dual agency" mentioned earlier, and Jesus's rejection of "traditionalism" excludes this idea. Neither does it mean: "Heaven will ratify whatever decisions you make about binding and loosing." That is likewise incompatible with Jesus's rejection of the human pretense to "finality." One cannot hold, as Jesus does, that every human word is to be subordinated to the word of God while at the same time affirming human "finality" or "dual agency." Jesus's saying rather means: "You will bind and loose in accordance with the will of heaven by using these keys of my teachings." Thus Gundry: "God will not ratify at the last judgment what Peter does in the present age, but Peter does in the present age what God has already determined. In other words, Peter has received direction from God for his scribal activity. This direction consists in Jesus's teaching."[72] Jesus therefore does not refer to any further connection between heaven and earth except that Simon will bind and loose in accordance with the will of heaven by making use of the keys of Jesus's teachings that he will be given.

Why would Jesus be emphasizing the "success" of Simon's binding and loosing by using the keys of his teachings? One possible and likely answer is that he means to make an implicit comparison with the Pharisees. The Pharisees certainly did presume to "bind" and "loose" with the authority of heaven, but Jesus rejects them entirely. The comparison thus works as follows.

Jesus's rejection of the Pharisees is a major theme of Matthew's Gospel. He says for example that one must exceed their righteousness if one is to have any hope of seeing the kingdom of heaven (5:20). The implication is that the Pharisees themselves will never see that kingdom.[73] Jesus also blatantly and publicly disregards their teachings about what is and is not proper to do on the Sabbath (12:1–14). He entirely ignores their appeals to the traditions of the elders (15:1–9). He says that they prefer human

72. Gundry, *Matthew*, 335.
73. Evans, *Matthew*, 119.

traditions to the commandments of God (15:9). He calls them a "plant" that his Father has not planted and that "must be uprooted" (15:13).[74] He also says that they are blind guides of the blind (15:14). He says that one must beware of their teachings as of a contagion (16:6, 11–12). He says that they are hard-hearted (19:8). He also compares them to wicked tenants that illegitimately try to take over a vineyard that does not belong to them (21:33–46). He says that they close up the kingdom of heaven and forbid others from entering (23:13), and that the people they convert become twice the children of Gehenna that they are (23:15). Their theological and halakhic interpretations are nonsensical (23:16–22). He says that their priorities are entirely the opposite of what they should be (23:23–28). Finally, he says that they are the children of those who killed the prophets and that all the guilt for all the blood of all righteous people who have ever died must come upon them (23:34–36). Jesus consequently rejects the Pharisees entirely. He rejects not only their teachings but even the legitimacy of their claim to authority. His opinion is that "the Pharisees, the leaders of the Jewish people, are not truly part of God's planting."[75]

How then to understand what he means when he says: "The scribes and Pharisees sit on Moses's seat. Therefore do everything that they tell you and obey it, but do not act according to their works, for they talk but do not also do" (23:2–3)? Carson, France, and Charles Talbert appreciate that Jesus is very clearly being ironic and sarcastic.[76] This is quite evident in context. How could Jesus sincerely command obedience to the teachings of the Pharisees when he will go on to say that these teachings shut people out of the kingdom of heaven and make them into children of Gehenna (vv. 13, 15)? Or how could he seriously be respecting the position of authority of the Pharisees when he would openly disregard their teachings and authority on so many occasions? How could he seriously be proposing obedience to the teachings of persons who will end up killing the prophets, sages, and scribes that he will send to them (v. 34)? Or how could he seriously be enjoining deference to persons deserving of punishment for the blood of all the righteous who have ever lived (v. 35)? The discourse in this chapter is positively contemptuous of the Pharisees. Saldarini does not consider the possibility of an ironic reading and yet admits that "[s]uch approbation of the scribes and Pharisees is contrary to much of what Matthew teaches."[77] Carson is thus

---

74. Mitch and Sri, *Gospel of Matthew*, 195.

75. Carson, "Matthew," 350.

76. Carson, "Matthew," 473; France, *Gospel of Matthew*, 324; Talbert, *Matthew*, 257.

77. Saldarini, *Pharisees, Scribes and Sadducees*, 165.

more convincing when he says: "The reluctance of many scholars to admit that vv. 2–3 are biting irony overlooks the tone of much of this chapter."[78]

Mitch and Sri think that Jesus might be separating the Pharisees' own traditions from their work as expositors of the Law of Moses. Jesus would be admitting their authority when they speak from the written Law but not when they speak from their traditions.[79] They therefore attempt to show that Jesus nevertheless has some respect for the Pharisees' position of authority. But this reading is not convincing at all.

Leave to the side the fact that this reading would make Jesus seem to have lost control of himself. He would be starting his discourse with a recognition of the Pharisees' authority only to end it by saying that they are guilty of all the blood of all the righteous who have ever been killed in history (v. 35). This would mean that Jesus's discourse becomes unhinged at some point. Also leave to the side the further fact that Jesus does not say that one should obey the Pharisees when they teach from the Law but rather that one should do "whatever they teach you" (v. 3). Jesus could hardly have meant that his followers should accept only some of the things the Pharisees teach by using the phrase "whatever they teach you." Suppose in any case that Jesus is in fact acknowledging the Pharisees' authority so long as they are rightly expositing the Law of Moses. This is the same thing as denying that the Pharisees simply as such have any authority. There is thus no difference between this reading and the one proposed earlier. The Pharisees' particular traditions and "oral Torah" are precisely what make them to be Pharisees as distinct from Sadducees or Christians.[80] Anyone who denied the authority of the oral Torah was for that reason not a Pharisee. To deny them authority in these respects is thus to deny them authority as Pharisees *stricto sensu*, and to recognize their authority only in the proper exposition of the Law of Moses is to admit the point that only God's words as distinct from all human words are originally, infallibly, and irreversibly authoritative. Other persons apart from God only become authoritative to the extent that they are relating and bearing witness to God's words; human traditions whether "officially sanctioned" or not have no normative force *per se*. This is exactly the perspective being proposed in the present essay. Yet the Pharisees claimed further authority for themselves than this. This perhaps is why they are a plant that God has not planted and which had to be uprooted (15:13). Carson is thus worth quoting once more: "The reluctance of many

---

78. Carson, "Matthew," 474.

79. Mitch and Sri, *Gospel of Matthew*, 291n5.

80. Carson, "Matthew," 348.

scholars to admit that vv. 2–3 are biting irony overlooks the tone of much of this chapter."[81]

This attempt to preserve a sense of respect on the part of Jesus for the Pharisees' authority therefore fails. Taking him as speaking sarcastically and ironically seems more consistent with the depiction of Jesus's attitudes toward the Pharisees in Matthew's Gospel in general. He is not recognizing the Pharisees' authority, nor does he think they have any authority of themselves. He is at best advising his disciples to avoid making trouble with the Pharisees for the time being. Saldarini thus rightly summarizes Jesus's attitude by saying: "Scribes and Pharisees are seen as corrupt leaders who reject God and fail to lead the people properly."[82]

In mentioning "binding" and "loosing" to Simon, Jesus is making an implicit comparison with the Pharisees. He is saying in effect: "What you bind on earth by using the keys of my teachings will in fact have been bound in heaven. This is how you will be distinguished from the Pharisees who bound or loosed as they pleased." Such a reading in the light of a proposed comparison to the Pharisees is consonant with the theme of Jesus's anti-Pharisaical polemic which is so dominant in Matthew's Gospel. It also agrees with the remarks about the Pharisees that Jesus makes toward the beginning of this same chapter. He says that the Pharisees are "an evil and adulterous generation" who do not know how to read the signs of the times and will receive no sign but the sign of Jonah (16:1–4). One must beware of their teachings as of a contagion akin to yeast (16:5–12). And he later goes on to say that he will suffer at the hands of the elders, chief priests, and scribes (16:21), in which group Pharisees are implicitly included. It is therefore contextually more appropriate to understand Jesus to be making an implicit comparison between Simon and the Pharisees: "Whatever you bind on earth (unlike them) will actually have been bound in heaven."

How does Simon "bind" and "loose"? By relating the teachings of Jesus to others. He will "bind" and "loose" in accordance with the will of heaven by relating Jesus's teachings which truly open and shut the kingdom of heaven to others.[83] Whatever these teachings forbid is "bound," and whatever they permit is "loosed." Whoever rejects these teachings is "bound" and the kingdom of heaven is closed to him or her, whereas whoever accepts them is "loosed" and the kingdom opened. This is how the "binding" and "loosing" take place: by teaching others to obey the commandments of Jesus. The authority that the Pharisees thought they had will actually be practiced by

---

81. Carson, "Matthew," 474.

82. Saldarini, *Pharisees, Scribes and Sadducees*, 165.

83. Blomberg, *Matthew*, 254; Gundry, *Matthew*, 336.

Simon so long as he propagates Jesus's own originally and infallibly authoritative teachings. As Carson says: "Whatever [Simon] binds or looses will have been bound or loosed, so long as he adheres to that divinely disclosed gospel. He has no direct pipeline to heaven, still less do his decisions force heaven to comply; but he may be authoritative in binding and loosing because heaven has acted first."[84]

Consider further the case of two other texts in the New Testament. Jesus repeats the same promise about "binding" and "loosing" in Matt 18:18 after a discussion of how to deal with one's offenders in the church. Likewise, he tells his disciples after the resurrection in John's Gospel: "Receive the Holy Spirit. If you forgive anyone's sins, their sins are forgiven; if you do not forgive them, they are not forgiven" (John 20:22–23). The same readings can be given here as earlier.

Jesus cannot really be taken as meaning in the Johannine text that whether or not anyone's sins are forgiven depends on the whim of the apostles. Otherwise they could forgive the sins of the whole world or else withhold forgiveness even from properly penitent persons. God would be leaving himself and the whole world at the mercy of the apostles. One might therefore be inclined to think instead that there must be certain conditions which stipulate when it is or is not appropriate for an apostle to announce the forgiveness of sins. But the stipulation of such prior conditions presumably depends upon God's teachings or expectations. For example, one must be properly penitent and have renounced behaviors contrary to the commandments of God and of Jesus. The apostles themselves in turn must be concerned to determine whether these conditions have obtained in the case of any person. This therefore means that the apostles are not so much forgiving sins themselves as they are announcing the prior forgiveness of a person's sins on behalf of God himself in the cases where these conditions obtain. This is consequently the meaning of Jesus's teaching: not that the apostles have a free authority to forgive or withhold sins, but rather that they are charged by Jesus with appropriately announcing the forgiveness of sins in keeping with the guidance of his teachings.

Something similar can be said in the case of the Matthean text as well. There Jesus is clear: "If your brother or sister sins against you, etc." (Matt 18:15). The apostles therefore are evidently not permitted to "bind" or "loose" as they please. They are rather to seek reconciliation with a person who has sinned. Yet they do not themselves determine what is or is not sin. This is determined by God and by Jesus's teachings. A thing is not a sin simply because the apostles or even any person is offended by it, as for

84. Carson, "Matthew," 373.

example Jesus's eating with sinners and tax collectors was not wrong simply because it offended the Pharisees. A thing is a sin rather because God and Jesus have forbidden it. The task of the apostles is therefore merely to bear witness to what Jesus and God have taught and thus to seek the restoration of the offending brother; they appeal not to their own authority but to the authority of Jesus's teachings in order to "bind" or "loose" in the church. This is why Jesus promises that what they will bind or loose will have been bound or loosed in heaven: because they will be guided by the heavenly teachings of Jesus rather than their own mistaken imaginations (as in the case of the Pharisees).

A final thing is worth noting here. The interpretation of the *petra* as Jesus rather than Simon makes it possible to discern a certain chiastic pattern in Matt 16:17–19. This Matthean passage spanning verses 17–19 begins and ends with statements apparently having to do with Simon. One might suppose for that reason that verse 18 is also about Simon, but this would in fact be a *non sequitur*. It is possible to propose instead that there is a chiasm: the first and last verse can be about Simon in relation to Jesus, while the center verse is principally about Jesus himself. The most important point of the chiasm is Jesus as the *petra* on which the church is built and against which the gates of Hades will not prevail. The statements about Peter would then be put in relation to a central and more important statement about Jesus. The structure of the chiasm is as follows:

> (A) 17 Blessed are you, Simon bar Jonah, for flesh and blood has not revealed [this] to you but my Father in the heavens.
>> (B) 18 And I say to you that you are *Petros* = of (the) *petra*,
>>> (C) and on this *petra* = on myself I will build my church, and the gates of Hades will not prevail against it = against me.
>> (B′) 19 And I will give you the keys of the kingdom of heaven = my teachings,
> (A′) and whatever you bind on earth will be bound in heaven, and whatever you loose on earth will be loosed in heaven.

This chiasm thus begins with a statement about Simon's God-granted knowledge of the true status of Jesus as Messiah (A). It then proceeds to a recognition of Simon's (new?) status or name as *Petros* in virtue of the confession he has made (B). The most important idea here is that Jesus is the *petra* from which *Petros* is named. The church is founded on Jesus as the *petra* against which the gates of Hades will not prevail because he will rise from the grave (C). The discourse then returns to a statement about Simon's newfound authority and significance as suggested by the mention of the "keys" (B′). Finally, it terminates with a statement about the use that Peter will make of these "keys" in accordance with his knowledge of Jesus's true status (*A'*). There is consequently this chiastic structure discernible in the text. It begins with two statements having to do with Simon's knowledge of Jesus's identity as Messiah: that it was revealed to him by God and that he is *Petros* in virtue of it. It then climaxes with two statements about Jesus: that he is the foundation of the church and that he will conquer the gates of Hades. It finally terminates with two statements about the way in which Simon will practically make use of his knowledge of Jesus's identity in the world: that he will receive the keys of the kingdom of heaven and that by using them he will bind and loose in accordance with God's will. Simon is granted knowledge about Jesus by God and a name which implies a relation to Jesus. This Jesus himself is the foundation of the church and the conqueror of Hades. And Jesus will give Simon his teachings by which he will exercise theological authority in the world with the agreement of God.

SUMMARY OF THE ARGUMENT

It has been argued thus that Jesus rejected "hierarchy." He says that all his disciples should think of themselves as brothers and equally students of the Messiah (Matt 23:8–10). This means that no one apart from God and Jesus can exercise theological authority in such a way as not to be open to questioning or correction principle. Every other person only exercises the derivative theological authority of fallibly and in principle reversibly relating and bearing witness to others the teachings and commandments of Jesus and the works of God in him. These teachings of Jesus are the "keys" by which the kingdom of heaven can be opened up or closed to others; these "keys" alone can be used to bind or loose in such a way as to guarantee agreement with heaven (16:19). This is because they are the teachings of Jesus the Son of God, and he alone knows God the Father and is capable of revealing him to others (11:27). The apostles of Jesus thus received no other authority from him than that of propagating his commandments to the world and teaching others to obey them (28:18–20). They exercise legitimate and successful authority when they pass on these teachings, whereas their authority is illegitimate or failed if either of these conditions do not obtain.

This also makes it possible to understand how Jesus can tell the disciples that he will "confer a kingdom on them" so that they will "eat and drink at his table" and "sit on thrones judging the tribes of Israel" (Luke 22:29–30). These words have nothing to do with "traditionalism" or "hierarchy." In other words, they have nothing to do with the apostles being set up in a position of special and privileged authority over everyone else in the church. They rather refer figuratively to the historical activity of the apostles in the church and the world after Jesus's resurrection as recounted in Acts. The "kingdom" conferred upon them is the kingdom that belongs to every person who accepts Jesus's teachings: the kingdom of God. The "eating and drinking" at the table of Jesus is the triumphant remembrance of his passion and celebration of his resurrection in the Eucharist. Finally, the "thrones" and "judgment of the twelve tribes of Israel" refer to the apostles' interactions with the Jewish hierarchies in the Acts of the Apostles. They "judge" the twelve tribes of Israel because they preach the gospel of the risen Jesus to massive crowds of Jews gathered from all over on the day of Pentecost (Acts 2:14–36). They also condemn the Council as opposed to the will of God (4:19–20, 5:29–30). They thus share in Jesus's kingdom and throne when they preach his word to others. And this interpretation is consistent with the rejection of "traditionalism" and "hierarchy."

5

Case Studies in Apostolic Authority

RECAPITULATION OF THE ARGUMENT

THIS BOOK HAS PUT forth an argument for a "low" view of ecclesial authority in matters of theology. The thesis has been that God and Jesus alone exercise original, infallible, and in principle irreversible theological authority in the church. All other persons exercise the derivative theological authority of fallibly and in principle reversibly relating and bearing witness to the teachings of Jesus and the works of God in him. The argumentation of the previous two chapters served to clarify further exactly what this means. The authority of all others in the church is "derivative" in the sense that they have no further theological authority than that of relating and bearing witness to what Jesus himself taught and what God has done in Jesus. Their words only have theological authority to the extent that they are also the words of Jesus or of God; God and Jesus speak for themselves and human beings have the responsibility of testifying truthfully to what they have said. The authority of all others in the church is "fallible" and "reversible" in the sense that no one is promised or guaranteed that he or she will teach and speak correctly except insofar as he or she is relating Jesus's teachings. This also means that no later generation of the church is necessarily beholden to the convictions, opinions, and practices of an earlier generation except to the extent that it judges these also to be the implicit or explicit teachings of Jesus.

This perspective was proposed in opposition to two ideas about theological authority in the church which were historically quite popular. These were here called "traditionalism" and "hierarchy." "Traditionalism" is the idea that some particular generation of a group can in principle make a binding and definitive decision about the practice or beliefs of the group on pain of exclusion. This decision therefore determines the identity of the group going forward so as to impose a "traditionalist" and retrospective deference to the past on the part of future persons who would want to be a part of it. "Hierarchy" is the idea that certain members within a group have the right and standing in principle to exercise unquestioned and un-corrected authority over others. These two ideas are closely related to each other. The kind of authority over the identity of the group presupposed by "traditionalism" is buttressed by the kind of authority over other members of the group at play in "hierarchy." These decisions made about the identity of the group can be said to be "binding" and "definitive" precisely because they were made by persons who occupy the appropriate rank within the hierarchy of the group.

"Traditionalism" and "hierarchy" are ideas found in the religious un-derstanding of the Pharisees. They are also found in contemporary Roman Catholic theology. But Jesus rejects both ideas, and this is especially clear in Matthew's Gospel. He rejects "traditionalism" because he thinks that every human word must always be measured against the more ultimate standard of God's word. This is evidenced through his rejection of the tradition of the elders regarding ritual handwashing as well as in the critique of the Pharisees' teaching about consecrating money to God (Matt 15:1–9). His polemic implies that human words and God's words are always distinct and separable, since only thus can they be compared. God speaks for himself, while human words are theologically authoritative only to the extent that they manage successfully to relate and bear witness to the divine words. The word of God cannot be confused with or blended into the word of a human. This means that no human authority is "final" as God is. It also means that there is no promise of providential guidance to support a pretense to infal-libility and irreversibility in matters of theological authority. Jesus likewise rejects "hierarchy" because he teaches that his disciples are all brothers and fellow students of the Messiah as their one teacher (23:8–10). He alone can expect the unquestioning obedience of his students, and he does not grant anyone in his church the authority to do anything except to pass on his teachings to others in order to make them disciples of Jesus (28:18–20). Robert Gundry explains this by saying that "Matthew democratizes scribal authority."[1] No one in the church has authorization from Jesus himself to

---

1. Gundry, *Matthew*, 336.

impose his or her own opinions or preferences on others as a matter of their friendship with God.

There are a few texts in the Gospels which initially seemed to demand an interpretation along the lines of "traditionalism" and "hierarchy." These include Luke 22:29–30 and Matt 16:17–19. But closer investigation revealed that it was not only possible but also desirable to read these texts in a way consistent with the rejection of "traditionalism" and "hierarchy" in the church. Jesus was not making Simon to be the "rock" on which he would build the church (Matt 16:18), neither was he granting Simon a kind of superior authority as "chief steward" and "second-in-command" within the church. Simon was called "Peter" (*Petros*) because he is "of (the) rock" in virtue of his confession of Jesus as the Messiah. Jesus is himself the rock (*petra*) on which he will build his own church. Simon is called *Petros* after Jesus the *petra*, just as Christians are named "Christians" after Christ in whom they believe. The gates of Hades will not prevail against this rock because he will rise from the dead, and upon rising he will give Simon the "keys of the kingdom of heaven" (16:19) in the sense that he will send him out into the world to make disciples of all nations by converting them to Jesus's teachings (28:18–20). The "keys" are themselves these teachings by which the kingdom of heaven is opened or closed to people who variously accept or reject them. These "keys" bind and loose in accordance with the will of heaven because God actually does approve or reject the very things Jesus teaches for or against. Simon will thus bind or loose what will have been bound or loosed in heaven (16:19) so long as he is propagating the teachings of Jesus. And all the apostles are figuratively said to "sit on thrones" and "judge the tribes of Israel" (Luke 22:30) when they go out into the world to preach the gospel of Jesus as described in Luke's Acts of the Apostles.

The thesis is therefore clear. The arguments in favor of it on the basis of explicit texts in Matthew's Gospel and the greater New Testament are clear, too. It is likewise clear that the rejection of the Pharisees for their "traditionalism" and "hierarchy" also implies the rejection of Roman Catholicism for the same reasons. What remains to be done here is for certain important episodes in the New Testament's depiction of the apostles and their use of authority to be interpreted in keeping with the idea that God and Jesus alone in the church exercise theological authority in an original, infallible, and in principle irreversible way.

THE QUESTION OF GENTILE CONVERTS

Perhaps the most significant theological crisis of the earliest generation of the church was the question of gentile believers. Were they to be welcomed into the church as gentiles, or must they first become Jews by being circumcised and committing to taking on the burden of the Law of Moses? The apostles eventually decided that gentiles could be welcomed simply as Gentiles; they did not first need to become Jews. It will be instructive to consider how exactly they came to this conclusion.

Stephen was brought before the council and accused by some persons of having taught that "this Jesus of Nazareth will destroy [the temple] and change the customs that Moses handed down to us" (Acts 6:14). Thus, already in the early days of the church some intuited that Jesus's teachings would require a radical rethinking and reevaluation of the principles of Jewish religion. Adolf von Harnack summarizes the notion by saying that "Christ had awakened among his personal disciples a faith in himself, which was dearer to them than all the traditions of the fathers."[2] This is arguably because Jesus claimed an authority and privilege for himself that relativized the whole system of Jewish religion. He was not subordinated to it but rather it to him. He opposes the Pharisees as the popular interpreters of Jewish religion in his day (Luke 6:1–5). He was of course not the only Jew to do this, but the precise way in which he did oppose the Pharisees implied a radically different conception of the place of Torah in one's relationship with God. For example, David Garland comments about Jesus's rejection of purity laws: "The dismissal of Pharisaic dietary laws is the prelude to the disciples' mission to all the nations."[3] And John Bowker explains the point as follows:

> What was particularly unwelcome to the Pharisaioi was [Jesus's] claim (as much in action as in word) that the action of God in the world of his creation can be made possible simply by the expectation, or faith, that it will be so, not necessarily by making that faith visible through the acceptance and observance of Torah, both written and interpreted. . . . Jesus . . . appeared to be claiming that the effect of God, the relation of God to a human situation, is possible even where no attempt at all is being made to accept and implement what God has commanded in Torah: sin can apparently be forgiven by a word (Mk. ii.1–12). Jesus did not necessarily deny the observance of Torah . . . but he certainly resisted the view that its observance is an indispensable

2. Harnack, *Outlines of the History of Dogma*, 22.
3. Garland, *Reading Matthew*, 164.

and prior condition of the action of God; faith is, if anything, the prior condition.[4]

Jesus thus saw God as accessible to faith apart from obedience to Torah. And there are further examples available as well. Jesus says that "the Son of Man is lord over the Sabbath" (Luke 6:5). His words in particular are like a rock (*petra*) on which one can build one's life and withstand any storm (6:46–48), and he interprets all the things in the Law and the Prophets in accordance with him and with what happened to him (24:27). The supremacy and ultimacy that Jesus claims for himself, together with the uneasy relationship in which he stood relative to the contemporary authorities at various levels, could thus have motivated the idea that to be a disciple of his can mean something other than being a Jew. He is more important than the Judaism of his day; God is accessible through him apart from the more specific concerns of the contemporary Judaism. This is also likely what Jesus means to refer to in his discourse to the disciples in the Gospel of John: "When the Spirit of truth comes, he will guide you into all the truth" (John 16:13). This Gospel was written some time after the gentiles had already been welcomed into the church.[5] The conflict between Jesus and "the Jews" referenced sixty times in that Gospel is therefore retold precisely in the light of the lesson the apostles had to learn in this first generation of the church: that faith in Jesus is greater and more important than obedience to the Torah as understood by their contemporaries. Thus Bowker once more: "Fundamentally, the offense of Jesus . . . lay in his attitude toward the various sources of authority, since in many different ways he claimed and exemplified direct authority, and power, from God."[6] And in noting "Jesus's insistence on the immediate reality of God to faith" which led to the conclusion that "even Torah was less important than faith and the realization of God to which faith can lead," Bowker also writes: "It was the resurrection which confirmed for [Christians] the validity of the way which Jesus had opened up to the reality of God, and which ultimately made it inevitable that Judaism and Christianity would become separated ways."[7]

Consider then what happens later. Sometime after the episode with Stephen's martyrdom Simon receives a vision from God. A sheet with various sorts of unclean animals drops down before him from heaven and he is told by a heavenly voice: "Rise, Peter, kill and eat" (Acts 10:13). He refuses to eat them, since they are unclean according to the Law. They cannot be eaten.

4. Bowker, *Jesus and the Pharisees*, 43.
5. See Bernier, *Rethinking the Dates of the New Testament*.
6. Bowker, *Jesus and the Pharisees*, 42.
7. Bowker, *Jesus and the Pharisees*, 52.

But after that he is rebuked: "That which God has made clean, you must not call profane" (v. 15). This happens three times. The vision thus suggests that the categories of the Law are now being superseded. Simon is then told by the Holy Spirit that he must descend to see some guests that have arrived at his house in search of him (vv. 19–20). He follows them the next day to Cornelius's house where he says: "You all know that it is unlawful for a Jewish man to associate with or draw near to a foreigner. Yet God has shown me that I am not to call any person 'profane' or 'unclean'" (v. 28). They then receive the Holy Spirit as he goes on to preach the gospel to them (vv. 34–46). Simon and his associates are shocked at this. He says: "Can anyone refuse the water of baptism to these who have received the Holy Spirit just as we did?" (v. 47). And so the gentiles are baptized in the name of Jesus (v. 48).

Simon is later called into question by certain Jews from Jerusalem associated with the church. They bring this accusation against him: "You went to uncircumcised men and ate together with them" (11:3). Simon then explains the situation to them from the beginning. He relates the vision, the visitors, the direction of the Holy Spirit, and the way the gentiles received the Holy Spirit upon his preaching the gospel to them (vv. 4–15). He says: "I remembered the word of the Lord, how he said: 'John baptized with water, but you will be baptized in the Holy Spirit.' If then God gave them the same gift as he gave to us when we believed in the Lord Jesus, who was I that I could get in God's way?" (vv. 16–17). They are impressed by the story and say: "Then even to the gentiles has God granted the repentance that leads to life!" (v. 18).

Certain persons later go from Jerusalem to the various places where Paul and Barnabas had had missionary success with the gentiles. They teach the converts: "Unless you are circumcised in keeping with the custom of Moses, you cannot be saved" (15:1). A dispute breaks out between these persons and Paul and Barnabas. Then they are sent to Jerusalem to discuss the matters with "the apostles and the elders" (v. 2). The Christians who were "of the sect of the Pharisees" maintained that the gentile converts "must be circumcised and commanded to keep the Law of Moses" (v. 5). The apostles and the elders gather together to debate the issue. Then Simon rises "after much debate" and tells the story of the vision and his experiences at the household of Cornelius (vv. 7–9). He points to the agency of God in the matter: "God, the one who knows the heart, bore testimony to them by giving the Holy Spirit to them just as to us and did not distinguish between them and us in purifying their hearts by faith" (v. 8–9). To impose obedience to the Law on them would be a matter of "testing God" (v. 10). This is especially evident because neither the Jewish Christians themselves nor their ancestors have been able to keep the Law. Simon's conclusion is therefore a clear and easy one: "We believe that we will be saved by the grace of the Lord Jesus in the same way as they" (v. 11). Silence comes upon the entire congregation. James pronounces his general agreement with Simon's position and proposes imposing no further burden upon the gentiles than a few simple rules (vv. 19–20). The apostles and elders of the church of Jerusalem then compose a letter to be sent to the gentile believers in Antioch, Syria, and Cilicia communicating the conclusions they have reached (vv. 23–29). Paul, Barnabas, Judas, and Silas deliver the letter and it is received with much rejoicing (vv. 30–32).

How does this episode in the early history of the church illustrate the theological authority exercised by the apostles? The most notable dimension of the narrative is that Simon and the apostles do little more than to point to what God has done through the preaching of the gospel of Jesus. They do not claim any authority of their own; they do not appeal to any rights they might possess, but only to what God has been doing and showing apart from their will.[8] They do not claim to be making it now possible for gentiles to become Christians apart from becoming Jews. They are only trying to be faithful to the manifest and public will of God in this matter and to submit to it. In the words of Luke Timothy Johnson: "Peter's role here is not as a 'prince of the apostles' but as another faithful witness whose function is to narrate his experience and draw implications from it."[9] Simon thus refers to the way he was sent by the Holy Spirit to Cornelius by saying: "You know that from the early days God made a choice among you that by my mouth the Gentiles should hear the word of the gospel and believe it" (v. 7). He also points to how God "made no distinction" between them and the gentiles by giving Cornelius and his household the Holy Spirit all the same (v. 8). Simon was not to discriminate against the gentiles "because God himself made no fundamental distinctions between peoples."[10] And it is not only Simon who reasons by making appeal to what God has clearly done. James likewise writes in his letter: "It has seemed good to the Holy Spirit and to us" (v. 28). He means by this that it seems consistent with what the Holy Spirit has done and with what the apostles have determined not to impose the whole burden of the Law upon the gentile converts.

Notably, it is rather the Pharisee Christians who had brought forth a thesis that Jesus himself never proposed. Johnson makes note of the "assumption of authority" on the part of the Pharisees.[11] They are perhaps still

---

8. Nemes, "Against Infallibility," 39–42.

9. Johnson, *Acts of the Apostles*, 261.

10. Johnson, *Acts of the Apostles*, 262.

11. Johnson, *Acts of the Apostles*, 260.

thinking in "traditionalist" and "hierarchical" terms. But the Messiah never taught that all converts to him must be circumcised and take up the burden of the Law of Moses. He only taught that they should take up the "light yoke" of his own teachings (Matt 11:28–30). And the gentiles to whom Simon preached received the Holy Spirit when they showed a genuine openness to the teachings and way of Jesus in the preaching of the gospel. The apostles therefore did nothing but call attention to what God himself had taught them by a clear and publicly attested experience: the saving relationship with God is founded upon faith in Jesus and not upon being a Jew who observes the Law of Moses.

This matter of the status of gentile believers was among the most important theological controversies to strike the church in its infancy. It is therefore all the more notable that the way in which the apostles treated it is in every way consonant with the notion that their own theological authority is only ever derivative, fallible, and reversible in principle. They do not claim to be teaching from themselves, and they never draw attention to the fact of their status. They only ever bear witness to what God or Jesus has taught independently of them. And it is especially notable that no reference is ever made to this "council" when this issue of "Judaizing" is brought up again in other places. Paul never argues from the authority of a council in any epistle of his.[12] He never justifies his attitudes towards gentile conversion by appeal to it. (Neither does he ever repeat the rules laid down by James in his own epistles, interestingly enough.) He only ever appeals to Scripture and to the experience of believers themselves. He appeals to Scripture: "The Scripture foreknowing that God would justify the Gentiles by faith, it declared the gospel beforehand to Abraham: 'All the nations shall be blessed in you'" (Gal 3:8). And he appeals to experience: "Did you receive the Spirit by the works of the Law or by listening with faith? Are you so stupid? Having begun in the Spirit, are you now going to be perfected in the flesh?" (vv. 2–3). Scripture itself teaches that justification comes by faith and not by the works of the Law, and every person's experience is that of receiving the Holy Spirit upon believing the gospel and not by performing works of the Law.[13] Craig Keener thus comments: "The Spirit is the nonnegotiable mark of true followers of Jesus, as members of God's eschatological people. As in Luke's account of Cornelius in Acts 10–11, so here the gift of the Spirit to gentiles confirms that God has already accepted them."[14] Paul's only method is therefore to bear witness to what God has said or done apart from him, whether in Scripture

12. See Johnson, *Acts of the Apostles*, 269–70.

13. Moo, *Galatians*, 182.

14. Keener, *Galatians*, 122.

or in experience. He does not appeal to a council or to his own authority as an apostle as a basis for establishing his theological opinions.

This episode of the "council of Jerusalem" thus serves to confirm the thesis of the present work. The apostles do not act as if they possess any authority of their own, they do not confuse their own words with the words of God, and they do not claim that God is speaking through them. They understand that their only authority is that of pointing to what Jesus or God has taught. They accept the gentiles into the church simply as gentiles because God himself has accepted them in giving them the Holy Spirit. Indeed, one could say that the gentiles were never required first to become Jews in order to become Christians, God himself deciding this point definitively by giving them the Holy Spirit apart from any such submission to the Law of Moses. The apostles at the council merely recognized God's own independent and binding action in this matter. Johnson thus writes that "the decision by James emphatically agrees with the perception of Peter, Paul, and Barnabas, that God was at work in the Gentile mission and that the Church must respond obediently to God's initiative."[15] The apostles and the church are merely following God's lead; this is how they are led by the Spirit into "all the truth" (cf. John 16:13). They never appeal to their authority as apostles or to the status of the "council" at Jerusalem to justify their opinions, and it is rather the Pharisees who attempt to impose an opinion with no basis in Jesus's words by insisting that the gentile converts be circumcised and take up the burden of the Law of Moses. This all resonates with the thesis that all persons in the church apart from God and Jesus have no further theological authority than that of fallibly and in principle reversibly relating and bearing witness to the teachings of Jesus and the works of God in him.

STEWARDS OF GOD'S MYSTERIES

The church in Corinth was suffering from a number of problems. This is evident in Paul's two epistles written to it. The first epistle especially deals with the problems of factions and divisions. Paul's response to this problem is precisely to point away from merely human authorities and to reorient the focus of the churches on Jesus himself. It will be worth considering this point in some detail.

Paul opens his first epistle to the Corinthians by appealing to unity in the light of some news he has received from some friends: "Now I appeal to you, brothers, through the name of our Lord Jesus Christ, that you all say the same thing and that there be no divisions among you, but that you be

15. Johnson, *Acts of the Apostles*, 272.

united in the same mind and the same purpose. For it has been reported to me by Chloe's people that there are quarrels among you, my brothers and sisters" (1 Cor 1:10–11).[16] What are these quarrels? They are quarrels about each person's preferred teacher: "What I mean is that each of you says, 'I am of Paul,' or 'I am of Apollos,' or 'I am of Cephas,' or 'I am of Christ'" (v. 12). The problem of disunity is thus a problem of misplaced allegiances and loyalties. The Corinthians made distinctions among the apostles and prominent figures of the early church, some preferring this teacher while others preferred that one. Gordon Fee writes that "the whole church has fallen prey to a love for disputation, in which various members exalt themselves . . . by supposing that their wisdom has been taken over from one of their renowned leaders."[17]

There are a number of significant points to make here. First, one could for example make the case that the Corinthians would not have divided themselves along the lines of their preferred teachers if there had been any official or well-known hierarchical division among the apostles and early itinerant teachers. There certainly would be no basis for saying "I am of Paul" if everyone knew and acknowledged that Simon Peter was the head of the apostles. Neither would there be any sense in saying "I am of Apollo" if everyone knew that the twelve apostles of Jesus occupied a distinct and uniquely authoritative office in the church. This kind of differentiation of allegiances seems like it would more naturally arise in response to a group of teachers who are more or less considered each to be on a level with the others. The differences only arise because certain persons are more prominent than their peers in a way that resonates with some and not with others. The Corinthians were declaring allegiance to their preferred teachers just as people might declare loyalty to a preferred philosopher or sports team.[18]

What is most important for present purposes is the way that Paul responds to this problem. He calls attention away from the different teachers themselves to Jesus who is the true focus of Christian faith: "Has Christ been divided? Was Paul crucified for you? Or were you baptized in the name of Paul?" (v. 13). It can make no sense to declare allegiances to this or that teacher of Jesus when it is Jesus himself who died for all and in whose name each one was baptized. Christian faith is not a matter of being a student of Paul or of Apollo or of Cephas; it is a matter of faith in Jesus the Son of God. Keener thus comments that the messengers of the gospel "preach

16. Fee, *First Epistle to the Corinthians*, 54; Keener, *1–2 Corinthians*, 24.

17. Fee, *First Epistle to the Corinthians*, 59.

18. Keener, *1–2 Corinthians*, 24–25.

Christ, not themselves."[19] And Paul himself insists that he did not preach anything to the Corinthians except Jesus crucified (2:2). There was nothing particularly impressive about his way of speaking or his physical presence. The only power he had was the power of the gospel of Jesus and the working of the Holy Spirit that accompanies it (vv. 3–5). All of this therefore served the purpose of directing attention to God himself in Jesus and not to Paul or to any mere human person (v. 5).

The division of the Corinthians by means of different allegiances to human teachers is, for Paul, something "merely human" (3:4). It comes from the mind of a person who is not properly spiritual (vv. 1–3). Gordon Fee comments: "Their quarreling represents the old ways—living as mere humans."[20] A properly spiritual way of thinking would rather understand that Paul, Apollos, and the rest are mere "servants through whom you believed, just as the Lord granted to each" (v. 5). Paul says that he planted the seeds among the Corinthians while Apollos watered them, yet it was God alone who gave the growth. In the words of Fee, God is both "responsible for growth . . . and the owner of the field."[21] This therefore means that Paul and Apollos are nothing while God is everything (vv. 6–7). They share a common line of work in which "each one will receive his own wages according to his own labor" (v. 8). Paul, Apollos, and the rest are but "God's servants" working in the churches which are God's field (v. 9).

The "foundation" on which Paul builds "like a wise architect" is Jesus himself (vv. 10–11). He builds on this foundation by calling no attention to himself at all but only to what God has done in Jesus (cf. 2:2). Jesus is the foundation on which the church is built into a house of God. This was indeed the foundation laid by God himself (3:11). But admittedly not every person always builds on this foundation in the same way. Some persons may build with materials that will withstand the fire of judgment while others may not (vv. 12–15). Some persons build with gold, silver, and precious stones, while others build with wood, hay, and straw. Paul does not have the impression that everyone who preaches Jesus does so equally well. And yet he also insists that the differentiation among builders will become evident on "the Day" (v. 13). Keener thus comments that "only the final judgment will arbitrate decisively what was in the hearts of God's servants."[22] This differentiation of teachers is therefore a matter for God to judge.

---

19. Keener, *1–2 Corinthians*, 26.

20. Fee, *First Epistle to the Corinthians*, 128.

21. Fee, *First Epistle to the Corinthians*, 130.

22. Keener, *1–2 Corinthians*, 42.

It is impressive to note how Paul judges the difference between true and false wisdom in this matter. The wisdom of God is not the wisdom of the world (v. 19). God seemingly always acts in such a way as to undermine human wisdom: "He catches the wise in their craftiness" (1 Cor 3:19; cf. Job 5:13) and "The Lord knows the thoughts of the wise, that they are futile" (1 Cor 3:20; cf. Ps 94:11). From these evidences Paul then draws the conclusion: "Therefore let no one boast in human beings" (1 Cor 3:21). It is no part of divine wisdom to align oneself with any particular human teacher. It is also worth mentioning that Paul here echoes exactly the conception of the relation between human words and divine words that Jesus himself maintained against the Pharisees. The words of Apollos, Paul, and Cephas are human words, and they themselves are mere humans. God does not speak through them in such a way that the human and divine words are blended and inseparable. They are rather sent out as witnesses testifying to what God has done. They are attempting to relate and bear witness to the works of God to the Corinthians. To boast in any of them would therefore be to boast in a human being and not in the Lord (cf. 1:31).

Paul then summarizes his lesson as follows: "Let a man think about us in this way: as servants of Christ and stewards of the mysteries of God" (4:1). These images are profoundly consonant with the conception of things being proposed in the present book. A servant has no authority except that of fulfilling the commandments of his or her master, neither has a steward any authority except that of taking care of what has been left in his or her charge.[23] Neither servant nor steward are authorized to act or speak from themselves. Of themselves they are nothing; the authority of a servant or steward is only ever derivative, fallible, and reversible in principle. These very same things are being said about Paul and Apollos. Every person who is charged with preaching the gospel to others is a servant of Christ and steward of the mysteries of God, and any such person has no other authority than that of relating to others what has been taught by Jesus and done by God in him.

It is also impressive that Paul tells the Corinthians not to make judgments between teachers. Servants and stewards are expected to be faithful to their masters (v. 2), but it is all the same to Paul himself whether human beings judge him in this or that way. He does not even judge himself (v. 3)! It is the Lord alone who will judge him on that Day to which Paul made reference earlier (v. 4). Fee thus writes: "The only judgment that counts is the final eschatological judgment administered by Christ himself."[24] On

---

23. Fee, *First Epistle to the Corinthians*, 159.

24. Fee, *First Epistle to the Corinthians*, 161.

that day "the Lord comes, who will also illuminate the hidden things of the darkness and make manifest the purposes of all hearts, and then the approbation from God will be given to each" (v. 5). And so Paul insists that the Corinthians "do not judge anything before the time." All things will be made clear on the day of judgment by Jesus himself.

Thus, in Corinth too there was a controversy that pertained to the question of theological authority. The Corinthians had divided themselves according to a differentiation of allegiances to human teachers. Paul's response to this situation is instructive. He thinks it is human foolishness to do any such thing. He takes a twofold line of response. First, he calls attention to the fact that Christian faith is not a faith in this or that mere human teacher but rather in Jesus himself and through him in God. Christians are not baptized into Paul or Apollos but rather into the name of Jesus. Then he "flattens" any possible differences between celebrity teachers such as Paul, Apollos, and Cephas by calling them all servants of Christ and stewards of God's mysteries. There is nothing special about them in themselves. Their job is only to bear witness to what God has done for all of humanity in the life, death, and resurrection of Jesus; the day of judgment will clarify who of them built with gold, silver, precious metals, wood, hay, or straw. This is harmonious with the thesis of the present essay that in the church God and Jesus alone exercise theological authority in an original, infallible, and in principle irreversible way. All others have only the derivative authority of fallibly and in principle reversibly bearing witness to the teachings of Jesus and to what God has done in him. They are but "servants of Christ" and "stewards of God's mysteries."

WHAT WAS FROM THE BEGINNING

John's first epistle opens with these words: "What was from the beginning, what we have heard, what we have seen with our eyes, what we have looked at and our hands have touched" (1 John 1:1). He thus places himself within the class of Jesus's eyewitnesses, contrary to the opinion of Raymond Brown and George Parsenios.[25] John identifies himself as one who bears witness to a life that was with the Father and revealed only lately (v. 2).[26] He testifies to Jesus the Son of God the Father. Indeed, he explicitly identifies his task as that of sharing with others what Jesus first shared with him. His goal is that of passing on the teachings of Jesus, and he writes for the sake of inviting others into this same fellowship: "What we have seen and heard we declare

25. See Brown, *Epistles of John*, 159–60; Parsenios, *First, Second, and Third John*, 43–44.
26. Kruse, *Letters of John*, 51–52, 61; Yarbrough, *1–3 John*, 33.

to you as well, so that you may have fellowship with us, and our fellowship is with the Father and with his Son Jesus Christ" (v. 3).

John thus understands his authority to be that of passing onto others what he first heard from Jesus. He tries to make his human word a restatement of the divine word that he has heard elsewhere. He writes: "The message which we have heard from him we also pass on to you, namely that God is light and there is in him no darkness at all" (v. 5). This is the message that John received from Jesus, and it is also what he passes on to everyone else. Robert Yarbrough comments: "John speaks of the message that he and other apostles were commissioned to convey to those who did not have the direct experience of Christ that the Twelve did."[27] He thus does not speak from himself or ever claim any special authority for himself. John only appeals to the authority of Jesus's own teachings and testifies to them as a witness. This means that the disobedience to these teachings is not a disobedience to John so much as it is a disobedience to Jesus: "If we say that we have not sinned, we make him a liar and his word is not in us" (v. 10). The denial of sin is principally a denial of Jesus and not a denial of the apostles as Jesus's witnesses in the world. And John likewise calls attention to "the message that heard from the beginning, that we should love one another" (3:11). All the teaching of God to which John bears witness is in fact this: "This is his commandment, that we believe in the name of his Son Jesus Christ and that we love one another, just as he gave us the commandment" (v. 23).

It is true that John appears to appeal to his authority and that of the apostles when he says: "We are from God. Whoever knows God listens to us; whoever is not from God does not listen to us. By this we know the spirit of truth and the spirit of error" (4:6). This "we" would seem to be the same "we" that spoke in the beginning: "What we have heard, what we have seen with our eyes, etc."[28] One might therefore get the impression that John is appealing to the apostolic college or some such as a measure for determining between truth and falsity.[29] Would this not imply some notion of "traditionalism" or "hierarchy" in the church? Would it not imply that the apostles possess the privilege of "finality" or "dual agency"? In fact it does not. The apostles are authoritative as witnesses because they are speaking about things that they have experienced for themselves (1:1–3). Their authority is consequently not institutional or "hierarchical" but rather epistemic in nature: they are more reliable witnesses to things having to do with Jesus because they followed him around for so long and were witnesses of his

27. Yarbrough, 1–3 John, 48.

28. Yarbrough, 1–3 John, 229.

29. Compare Brown, Epistles of John, 508–10.

resurrection. This is therefore the sense in which the college of the apostles is the measure of truth and error.

One can certainly draw from John's epistle the notion that the apostles are especially authoritative witnesses to Jesus in the early church, but from this it does not follow that their authority is institutional or official in nature according to a notion of "hierarchy." Their testimony is authoritative because they bear witnesses to Jesus's teachings as ones who saw him, listened to him, sat and ate with him, and so on. They are bearing witness to what they have seen, heard, and held in their hands (1 John 1:1, 3; cf. John 3:11). The apostles exercise an authority that is derivative, fallible, and reversible in principle. Their only authority is that of bearing witness to the teachings of Jesus and the works of God in him. They do not have the right to do anything beyond that, nor do they claim for themselves anything beyond that. John is clear that he and the other apostles are but witnesses bearing testimony to something beyond them which enabled them to have fellowship with God and his Son.

SUMMARY OF THE DISCUSSION

The thesis of the present essay is once more that God and Jesus alone exercise original, infallible, and in principle irreversible theological authority. All other persons exercise only the derivative authority of fallibly and in principle reversibly relating and bearing witness to others about the teachings of Jesus and what God has done in him. This thesis was argued in the previous two chapters on the basis of Jesus's rejection of the "traditionalism" and "hierarchy" of the Pharisees in the Gospels. And this chapter's preceding cursory study of important discussions of apostolic authority in the New Testament has served to confirm the thesis.

The apostles did not take themselves to have any other theological authority than that of making disciples of Jesus by relating his teachings and bearing witness to the works of God in him. They met the theological problems they confronted in their various contexts by pointing away from themselves and back to the facts of the matter in Jesus's teachings or in the works of God in time. This is how they resolved the question of gentile converts to Christianity in the Acts of the Apostles. This was also the method of Paul in dealing with the factionalism of the Corinthians. There he was explicit that one should think of him and Apollos and indeed all teachers in the church as nothing more than servants of Christ and stewards of God's mysteries. They have no other authorization or task than that of bearing witness to what Jesus has taught and what God has done in him. And John also agrees with this conception of things in his first epistle. There he describes himself and the other apostles as persons who bear witness to the works of God which they have seen, heard, and experienced firsthand in Jesus. The evidence from the practice and teaching of the apostles as recorded in the New Testament therefore corroborates the argument of this book.

6

Objections

THE THESIS OF THIS essay has been argued on the basis of Jesus's words themselves. Case studies in the apostolic exercise of theological authority in the New Testament have been examined and found supportive of it. Taking for granted the cogency of the argument of the previous chapters, what remains to be done here is to respond to some objections that may be brought against it. Most of all, the thesis of the present essay will be seen to be quite consequential for the future and direction of Protestant theology. It will become evident in the end that if friendship with God is a matter of the fulfillment of the teachings of Jesus, then submission to the dogmatic pronouncements of past generations of the church catholic is not essential insofar as these doctrines cannot be definitively established on the basis of Jesus's teachings. This means that Christian faith and life is ethical, spiritual, and practical in nature, rather than dogmatic and speculative-metaphysical.

THE FOUNDATION OF THE APOSTLES

Does not the New Testament teach that the church is built on the foundation of the apostles and the prophets? This would appear to imply that they occupy a special position within the "hierarchy" of the church. Yet this seems to be a misunderstanding of the meaning of those texts.

Paul writes to the Ephesians that they are "members of God's family who are built on the foundation of the apostles and the prophets, Christ Jesus himself being the cornerstone" (Eph 2:19–20). But it is not at all obvious that he is referring to the church as a kind of institution. He rather says that the Ephesians themselves are "built" (*epoikodomēthentes*) on the foundation of the apostles and prophets. The passive participle is plural. This would be a way of referring to the fact that they learn about Jesus and are strengthened in their commitment to him by these sources. But the apostles and prophets can be the sources of one's knowledge about Jesus and his teachings without themselves occupying a certain rank within the church conceived as a "hierarchical" structure. They "build up" the Ephesians by their preaching and exhortations, and this is compatible with the apostles and prophets having no further authority than the derivative one of fallibly and in principle reversibly relating and bearing witness to the independent work of God and teachings of Jesus. This text therefore does not undermine the argument of this book.

Similar remarks can be made about the image of the "twelve foundations" of the bride of the Lamb on which are "the twelve names of the twelve apostles of the Lamb" (Rev 21:14). The apostles were witnesses of Jesus who had followed him from place to place. They learned from his own mouth his teachings about what a person must do and believe for the sake of friendship with God. They were then sent by Jesus into all the world to call all people to the obedience of Jesus's teachings and commandments. They laid the historical foundations of Jesus's church in the world. Harold Hoehner thus writes that these texts from Ephesians and Revelation indicate "that the apostles and the prophets are the historic persons who first formed the universal church."[1] They can in this sense be said to be the "foundation" of the bride of the Lamb conceived as a heavenly city, namely as its founders. But to say that the apostles possessed the kind of functionally original theological authority implied by the notions of "traditionalism" and "hierarchy" is entirely irrelevant to all this. There is no basis or need for making this additional supposition.

There is still a further point worth mentioning here. One of the disagreements between Protestants and Roman Catholics has to do with the question of "apostolic succession."[2] Much about this has been written elsewhere.[3] It will suffice to note the following point here. Irenaeus wrote that the apostles "delivered up their own place of government" in the church to the bishops (*Against Heresies* 3.3.1). Some persons with a "traditionalist" and "hierarchical" conception of the church might therefore conclude from this that the bishops have (nearly) the same "lofty" authority the apostles purportedly had: a theological authority that could on occasions be strictly

---

1. Hoehner, *Ephesians*, 399.

2. See the discussions in Sullivan, *From Apostles to Bishops*; Stewart, *Original Bishops*.

3. See Nemes, *Orthodoxy and Heresy*, ch. 3; *Theology of the Manifest*, ch. 5.

derivative and yet functionally original. But the argumentation of the present essay undermines this inference. It can be granted that the apostles left their place of government and authority to the bishops of the subsequent generation of the church. This means no more than that these bishops now have the work of passing on the teachings of Jesus to Christians in each congregation. It does not follow that the authority of the bishops is therefore "lofty," because their inherited apostolic authority is strictly derivative, fallible, and in principle reversible. The authority of the bishops is not "lofty" because the authority of the apostles themselves whom they succeed was not itself "lofty." As Huldrych Zwingli says: "The episcopate, that is, the ministry of the word, is an office, not a rank."[4] The question of apostolic succession must therefore be considered irrelevant to the debate between "high" and "low" views of ecclesial authority in theology.

THE AUTHORITY OF SCRIPTURE

If the theological authority of the apostles was derivative, fallible, and in principle reversible, does this not undermine the authority or infallibility or inerrancy of Scripture? No. The problem with this objection is that it equivocates on the notion of "fallibility" and confuses fallibility with error.

One must first notice an equivocation in the question. To say that Scripture is fallible generally connotes that it has errors. This is because Scripture already says what it will ever say. It has already spoken, and the ascription of "fallibility" to someone or something who cannot say anything further generally communicates the actuality of error. It would be an unwarranted ascription if a falsehood or error had not yet been established. But to say that the apostles were fallible after their commission by Jesus is to say that they were capable of error. This is because they had not already said everything they would ever say. Now the apostles were admittedly fallible. They were not assured ahead of time that they would always exercise their theological authority in a legitimate and successful way; no such promise was made to them. But from this fact alone it does not follow that they ever failed! It only follows that it was possible for them to fail in some respect or other. By way of example, suppose a man loves a woman. It is possible that she loves him back, but from this possibility it does not follow that she actually does. Or consider how it is always possible for a given boxer to lose a match. From this it does not follow that he ever loses. The possibility of a thing thus does not entail its actuality. So also, it was possible in principle for the apostles to make illegitimate or unsuccessful use of their theological

4. Zwingli, *Commentary on True and False Religion*, 257.

authority, yet from this alone it does not follow that this actually did happen at some point. Fallibility does not straightaway imply failure.

But suppose for the moment that the apostles did at times fail in their exercise of theological authority. Perhaps they occasionally imposed opinions or practices on their converts with a greater dogmatism than was merited, or perhaps not everything they passed on to their followers was strictly true. There is no reason to suppose this is impossible. Would it follow from this general possibility that therefore the reliability of Scripture is undermined? No.

The apostles all certainly did more things and wrote more letters or works than are included in the New Testament. There were more apostles than are found in the spotlight of the Gospels, Acts, and Epistles, and likely not everything they did was always noteworthy or successful. Yet one could nevertheless maintain that the documents constituting the New Testament were preserved precisely because the earliest Christians could sense that these works in particular were worth retaining. Consider how not everything a person ever writes or produces is judged worthy of publication by others, and yet some things are. Some manuscripts do not make it into print, and some paintings do not find their way to an exhibition or museum—but some do. These remain because they are better; they are good enough that the works themselves demand to be treasured. One could therefore say something similar about the apostles and their writings. The New Testament documents were judged worthy of publication by the church as a whole. The works themselves were sufficiently notable and useful as to motivate the conviction that they ought to be preserved and passed down; the church, which already had the faith apart from these documents, saw its faith expressed in these documents in an especially useful way and thus determined to keep them. This is a sense in which one could say that the New Testament texts are "self-authenticating."[5] They are self-authenticating precisely to the person who recognizes in them an authentic expression of his or her own Christian faith. One might even say that the church recognized their "inspiration."[6] That is therefore why they remained in the church despite the general fallibility of the apostles and of all other persons.

There is no reason to think that the apostles were always correct in everything they thought or did. Paul himself mentions a major blunder and mistake on Simon's part. He tells how Simon refused to sit to eat with gentile believers at Antioch out of fear of certain persons "of the circumcision" that visited the church from James (Gal 2:12). In this respect he left a

5. See the discussion of this matter in Kruger, *Canon Revisited*, ch. 3.

6. See Peckham, *Canonical Theology*.

bad example for other Jews and even for Barnabas, the partner of Paul who
followed him in his "hypocrisy" (v. 13). Paul therefore rebuked him "in the
sight of all" for failing to live up to the truth of the gospel (v. 14). It is clearly
pointless to try to draw a distinction between this sort of failing on Simon's
part and an erroneous "official statement." There is no reason in the New
Testament for thinking that Simon could ever make an "official statement"
of any kind. Jesus never told him about anything like that, nor does he have
an "office" for which such a thing is possible. There is still less reason for
thinking that Simon possessed any guarantee that he would be protected
from error in every "official statement" he makes. Once more, Jesus never
mentions any such thing. These ideas are founded in a reading of Jesus's
mention of the "keys" and the "binding" and "loosing" (Matt 16:19).[7] People
assume that Jesus must have been promising Simon the same kind of "hierarchical" authority that the Pharisees presumed to have, but this passage has
already been interpreted otherwise above. Simon's authority is only that of
bearing witness to the teachings of Jesus and the work of God in him. Paul
thus rightly rebukes him when he fails in this respect.

There is consequently no reason for affirming that the apostles were
anything but derivatively, fallibly, and reversibly authoritative. They were
but "servants of Christ" and "stewards of God's mysteries." They are not
themselves the objects of Christian faith, even if a Christian comes to faith
by means of their testimony. They are but witnesses to Jesus as faith's true
object. One could say that they do retrospectively what John the Baptist
did prospectively. John was sent to bear witness to the coming Messiah.
He came to point out the Messiah and to encourage everyone to believe in
him. The apostles likewise were sent to bear witness to the Messiah after he
had already come and accomplished the salvation of the world through his
death on behalf of all (cf.1 Tim 2:4–6; 1 John 2:2). They are thus no more
the objects of Christian faith than John the Baptist would be. Their goal in
preaching and teaching is simply to point to Christ. They must do as John
the Baptist said about himself: they must decrease while he increases (cf.
John 3:30).

Someone might wonder whether this conception of the development
of the New Testament canon would not undermine the notion of a "closed"
canon. Couldn't further works be added alongside the writings of the apostles if these were judged to be sufficiently valuable? There are a few points
to make in response.

First, one could say that this is effectively what has happened in those
traditions which grant functionally original (i.e., infallible and irreversible)

7. See Ott, *Fundamentals of Catholic Dogma*, 287.

authority to magisterial statements of the church, such as the definitions of ecumenical councils or of the bishop of Rome. These traditions admittedly will distinguish between inspired Scripture and authoritative commentary on or interpretation of Scripture, but the end result is the same: something distinct from the biblical canon is added alongside it as being functionally equal to and inseparable from it. The Roman Catholic Church accepts this consequence: "It is not from Sacred Scripture alone that the Church draws her certainty about everything which has been revealed. Therefore both sacred tradition and Sacred Scripture are to be accepted and venerated with the same sense of loyalty and reverence."[8] Official statements of sacred tradition have been collected (for example) in Heinrich Denzinger's *Sources of Catholic Dogma*.[9] There are consequently already traditions doing exactly what this inquiry mentions as objectionable.

Second, it must be noted that there is a certain epistemic privilege had by the apostles and this earliest generation of the church that is not shared by others.[10] The earliest generation of Christians and especially the apostles of Jesus were unique as witnesses to Jesus's teachings. They were his students; they learned from his mouth what he wanted from them. The goal of a Christian is therefore to learn from these persons and to identify with them. The goal is to become Christian precisely by becoming "apostolic." But this is best done by focusing one's attention on the apostles. Later generations of Christians also shared this same purpose in that they also wanted to be "apostolic." But there is no guarantee that they succeeded in every respect.[11] There is consequently no basis for according their writings and insights functionally the same authority as that of the apostles of Jesus themselves. This does not mean that they have no value whatsoever; they do not need to be rejected in every respect. But they do need to be held in a subordinate position. One's goal as a Christian is to become like Jesus, and this is best done by learning from him through his immediate students whom he personally commissioned to pass on his teachings.

FALLIBILITY AND THEOLOGY

Wouldn't the rejection of the infallibility of the apostles or of the church at large lead to religious skepticism? Thomas Joseph White writes: "If the Church cannot teach infallibly, then we are in fact required to say something

8. *DV* 9.

9. Denzinger, *Sources of Catholic Dogma*.

10. Cf. Weger, "Tradition."

11. See Hart, *Tradition and Apocalypse*.

absurd of just this kind[:] 'God has revealed himself, but the Church can never say with assurance what God has revealed.'"[12]

This objection is likewise confused. The presupposition of the church's preaching is not the infallibility of the church, but rather that Jesus or God has successfully communicated something to human beings which the church then passes on to others. But success of communication does not require infallibility. This much is obvious from everyday experience. Human beings regularly succeed in communicating with one another and manage to pass on the ideas of others despite the fact that no one is infallible. Thus, one can grant that apostles were fallible. This clearly does not mean that God and Jesus never succeeded in communicating with them! For that reason, too, it does not undermine the church's preaching.

How can successful communication take place? There are two ways to assure it. One way is for the hearer to be infallible. But another, more feasible way is for the speaker to accommodate him- or herself to the fallibility of the hearer by making the thing communicated simple enough and easy to grasp on its own. Human fallibility can be overcome by clarity and simplicity. Consider the following analogy with respect to nature. There is no infallibility among scientists; no scientist possesses an infallible interpretive insight into the "self-communication" of nature. Yet from this it does not follow that humanity is in a place of skepticism and ignorance as to whether water hydrates or fire burns or the sun warms! Some things are clear enough; they speak clearly from themselves. The same thing can therefore be said of Jesus's teachings. He communicates with success, not because his listeners are infallible, but because what he teaches is clear enough in itself.

CLARITY AND OBSCURITY

The suggestion made above was that the fallibility of human beings can be overcome by the clarity of what God and Jesus mean to communicate. The obvious rejoinder will be that not all the necessary things in theology are as simple and clear as that. What then can be said?

First, this opinion apparently was not shared by some very important figures in early Christian history. They thought that the essential things of the faith were in fact capable of being formulated clearly and plainly, that the apostles had so communicated them in their writings and in their preaching, and that this plain clarity of the teachings is precisely what makes the succession from the apostles to their contemporary bishops reliable.

12. White, *Light of Christ*, 37.

Consider the case of Origen of Alexandria. He writes: "Now, it ought to be known that the holy apostles, in preaching the faith of Christ, delivered with utmost clarity to all believers, even to those who seemed somewhat dull in the investigation of divine knowledge, certain points that they believed to be necessary" (*On First Principles* Preface 3). And he identifies these "certain points" as "the ecclesiastical preaching, handed down from the apostles through the order of succession and remaining in the churches to the present" (Preface 2). These are in the main the ideas presented in what today is known as the "Apostles' Creed" (with some exceptions): God as the source of one's life and creator of all things; Jesus as his only son and savior of humanity; and the Holy Spirit. Origen thus maintains that the essential things of the faith were explained simply and clearly by the apostles and were passed down in all the churches. It is these simple and clear teachings that constitute the substance of the preaching the churches.

This implies that the essential things of the faith can in fact be explained and presented "with utmost clarity." They are not condemned to be obscure or difficult to grasp from the start. But there is also a further implication worth noting. Origen could not be making this argument if the essential things were not simple and clear of themselves. Otherwise it would be ambiguous whether the teachings of the churches agree with the apostolic testimony as well as with each other. Only something simple and clear enough of itself can easily be recognized when it appears in different places; something that is easily confused for something else or difficult to understand is not easily discerned. The judgment of the reliability of the transmission thus presupposes the simplicity and clarity of the transmitted teachings. One could even say that it is precisely the clarity of the essential teachings of the faith that makes the succession from the apostles a reliable one, since it is not easy to "mess up" the transmission of something simple and clear on its own. Origen therefore asserts the clarity of the essential things.

Consider likewise Irenaeus of Lyons. He writes that "the entire Scriptures, the prophets, and the gospels, can be clearly, unambiguously, and harmoniously understood by all, although all do not believe them" (*Against Heresies* 2.27.2). He is convinced that anyone who reads the Scriptures "with attention" will find in them "an account of Christ" such as the apostles passed on in the churches (4.26.1). And he maintains that the church throughout the whole world has in fact received only one and the same faith from the apostles: once more, roughly the content of the "Apostles' Creed" (1.10.1), with notable overlap with what was listed by Origen. This is a part of his argumentation against the Gnostics.

The same point therefore holds here as in the case of Origen. Irenaeus thinks that the essential teachings of the Scriptures can be easily and unambiguously understood by all. He does not even think one has to be a believer in order to understand them. He likewise could not convincingly say that all the churches in the world received one and the same faith that one finds in the Scriptures unless this faith itself were simple and clear enough and susceptible of so clear a formulation as to be recognizable for what it is in various places. One could not speak so confidently of a shared faith if the faith itself were something obscure and unclear, since one would have to be able to compare the teachings of all the churches both amongst themselves and with the writings of Scripture. Neither could one judge that the transmission of the faith from one generation of teachers to the next were reliable unless the thing itself being passed down were clear and simple. And the only way for this comparison to be made in such a way as to warrant Irenaeus's confidence of identity of teaching is for these teachings to be simple and clear enough in themselves. It is once more precisely the simplicity and clarity of the essential content of the faith that makes the transmission reliable; only thus could he convince his gnostic opponents in argument by helping them see for themselves that all the churches teach the same thing.

Here then is the first point. The notion that the essential things are obscure or cannot be formulated clearly or easily found in Scripture is not present in the early generations of the church. If this is to overstate the point, then one can say that it is at the very least contrary to the opinions of Origen and Irenaeus. These early church figures both presuppose and straightfor-wardly assert not only that the essentials of the faith are susceptible of clear and plain formulation, but also that such formulations are to be found in Scripture and in the preaching of the apostles and their successors alike.

Yet there is still more to say. It may well be that the things which (say) Roman Catholicism in particular considers to be essentials of the faith are not as clear as that. They are not easily found in the pages of the Bible, nor are they easily found in the restatements of the "rule of faith" given by Origen and Irenaeus, nor are they readily discerned in the preaching of ev-ery generation of the church. Examples include the belief in the perpetual virginity of Mary, her immaculate conception, and her assumption into heaven. There is no simple and clear sentence in Scripture or the earliest sources asserting these ideas. One might think therefore that the obscurity of these ideas in the sources and the weakness of ordinary folk as interpret-ers must be supplemented by positing an infallible ecclesial magisterium. Brandon Dahm proposes something like this argument as playing a role in his conversion to Roman Catholicism.[13] Neal Judisch likewise offers

13. Dahm, "That Great Revolution of Mind," 99–100.

such reasoning when he recounts his own experience of the divisions
arising within the confessional Presbyterian churches in response to the
controversy about the "Federal Vision."[14] He writes that "our problem was
that while we had Scripture and (interpretive, confessional) tradition, we
lacked a recognizable authority who could adjudicate dogmatic disagreement (e.g., a magisterium)."[15] But this conclusion would not follow at all.
Another can also be drawn: namely, that these admittedly unclear and
undecidable things are not in fact essential to the faith. These ideas are not
easily found in the Bible or in the teachings of Jesus and the apostles for the
reason that the biblical authors were not concerned with them in the first
place and they play no part in the original preaching. Jesus does not teach
these things clearly because they have nothing to do with his message. One
could even parody White's argument and say that the proposal of a magisterium implicitly accuses Jesus of being incapable of communicating the
necessary things clearly.

Jesus did not bother to teach these purportedly necessary things so
clearly as to remove all doubt, but there certainly are teachings of Jesus
that are sufficiently clear on their own to be communicated effectively even
without the pretense of infallibility on the part of those who hear them.
These are that God, as the source of all things and of one's life, is one's Father; that one should trust in him; repent of one's sins; obey his commandments; love God with all one's heart; love one's neighbor as oneself; pray
without ceasing for all things in the expectation of receiving; treat others
as one would want to be treated; and so on. These things are clear enough,
and it is precisely these things that open up the kingdom of heaven to
people. Adolf von Harnack said it correctly: "Protestantism reckons—this
is the solution—upon the Gospel being something so simple, so divine, and
therefore so truly human, as to be most certain of being understood when it
is left entirely free, and also as to produce essentially the same experiences
and convictions in individual souls."[16] And elsewhere: "No! the Christian
religion is something simple and sublime; it means one thing and one thing
only: Eternal life in the midst of time, by the strength and under the eyes of
God."[17] And still elsewhere he references "the inner and essential features
of the Gospel—unconditional trust in God as the Father of Jesus Christ,
confidence in the Lord, forgiveness of sins, certainty of eternal life, purity

14. Judisch, "Of Towers and Tongues," 107–8.
15. Judisch, "Of Towers and Tongues," 108.
16. Harnack, *What is Christianity?*, 275; emphasis removed.
17. Harnack, *What is Christianity?*, 8.

and brotherly fellowship."[18] This is the true preoccupation of Jesus's teachings: a life reconciled with God one's Father and in harmony with others. He preaches the arrival of the kingdom of heaven in his person and the possibility of enjoying the life of that kingdom here and now through his teachings. But he never says two words about the immaculate conception of his mother or anything of the sort. Why then should anyone be positively obliged to believe things that cannot be clearly established by reference to Jesus's teachings? Why call an obscure thing necessary?

Grant that some portion of all the persons in the world who call themselves Christians are convinced that certain such speculative metaphysical opinions are essential to the faith. What is supposed to follow from this? One might think that this group is unjustly attempting to impose its opinions on others without an adequate basis in the teachings of Jesus, or claiming to speak on behalf of Jesus and thus to put itself on a par with him without being commissioned to do so, or even accusing Jesus of being incapable of communicating clearly and setting itself up as a necessary supplement to his incapacity as a teacher. And one might also think that these persons are more motivated by the concern that everyone submit to their preferred opinions and be like them, rather than by any actual submission on their part to what Jesus himself taught. Yet no one among mere humans has the pure right to demand that others think just like him or her. Only the truth as such demands to be believed, and the things that this particular group believes are by its own concession not clear and simple and thus not easily proven or demonstrated to be true from Jesus's own words. But Jesus does not give anyone the right to impose his or her own opinions on others; his commission was only that his own teachings be brought to all the nations (Matt 28:18–20). One can therefore argue that these presumptions to authority are a "plant" that God has not planted in the church and which must be uprooted (Matt 15:13).

FALLIBILITY AND ECCLESIAL CHAOS

One might wonder whether the denial of any special theological authority or infallibility to the apostles or to any other persons in the church makes room for anarchy and constant division and insubordination. But this would not follow at all. It has already been shown that the fallibility of human beings as recipients of God's teachings can be overcome by the clarity and simplicity of those teachings themselves. There need be no chaos in the church over the fact that people ought to pray to God for all things or do

18. Harnack, *What is Christianity?*, 180.

good to all people or that they have salvation through Jesus's death on their behalf. Ecclesial chaos is averted by emphasizing the clear things and allowing for differences of opinion about the obscure. But more can also be said.

Consider the following analogies. One's eyesight is not infallible, yet this does not mean one must always be questioning one's eyes. It is enough to take their reliability for granted and to make adjustments as the flow of one's experience demands. One's thinking is not infallible, yet this does not mean one must always be questioning one's judgments. It is enough to consider one's thoughts carefully and to be willing to revise them if circumstances should require it. One's feelings are not infallible, yet this does not mean that one must always be fighting against one's feelings. It is enough to take them seriously and to be willing to renounce them if they prove themselves unreasonable. One's parents are not infallible, yet this does not mean one must always contradict them. One's desires are not infallible, yet this does not mean one must never act on any desire at all. One's wife or husband is not infallible, yet this does not mean one should constantly contradict or undermine them in anything they say. Admitting fallibility therefore does not open the door for chaos. It only means being willing in principle to make course corrections.

The truth is that fallibility is an inevitable part of the human condition, and yet nothing could ever be accomplished unless a course of action were taken despite the unavoidable possibility of error. Being fallible thus means having to act with a measure of faith. Origen responded to Celsus's criticism of the Christian emphasis on faith by calling attention to the fact that everyone exercises a bit of faith anytime they engage in an undertaking they know may not necessarily succeed:

> Who goes on a voyage, or marries, or begets children, or casts seeds into the ground, unless he believes that things will turn out for the better, although it is possible that the opposite may happen—as it sometimes does? But nevertheless the faith that things will turn out for the better and as they wish makes all men take risks, even where the result is not certain and where things might turn out differently. (*Contra Celsum* 1.11)

Origen is clear that this is just the way things are for human beings. They have to act and yet cannot be sure that they are acting rightly; they have to believe something and yet cannot be sure that they are believing correctly. But admitting the possibility of error does not necessarily mean entering into a kind of paranoia or paralysis in which no one can be trusted and no action be undertaken at all. It only means not claiming more certainty for oneself than one actually has. It means admitting to the possibility of being wrong and of having to course correct. Living a human life always means stepping out into the unknown in faith; there is no other way for humans to be. And it is worth remarking that Origen acknowledges the appropriateness of this line of reasoning in matters of religion as well. There is no escape from fallibility even in religion.

THE ESSENTIALS OF THE FAITH

If the church is not conceived along "traditionalist" and "hierarchical" lines, how can it come to a definitive statement about what is and is not essential to the faith? How can theological disputes be resolved in a binding manner?

One should first admit that Jesus did teach certain things clearly. It is worth citing Harnack once more on "the inner and essential features of the Gospel—unconditional trust in God as the Father of Jesus Christ, confidence in the Lord, forgiveness of sins, certainty of eternal life, purity and brotherly fellowship."[19] Jesus taught for example that one must believe in him, that one must repent of one's sins, that God is one's Father who means to do one good in everything, that one must love God with all one's being, that one must love one's neighbor as oneself, that one must treat others as one would want to be treated by them, that one must pray for all things with faith and expectation, that one must welcome the stranger and visit the sick and imprisoned, and so on. Jesus taught a life reconciled with God one's Father and in harmony with others. These teachings are clear enough; indeed, they are clearer than one might think, given how little effort many Christians put toward fulfilling them. But leave this point to the side. This question about essentials assumes a particular understanding of the faith that must be called into question. More specifically, it assumes that being a Christian is a matter of believing very specific ideas or assenting to particular doctrines.

This would certainly apply to those things which Jesus taught clearly. One can hardly claim to be a Christian and refuse to believe in Jesus or to love God or one's neighbor. This would be a refusal to do what Jesus plainly demands. But the problem is that there are very specific ideas or doctrines that came in time to be considered essential to the faith *per se*, and yet these same ideas and doctrines are not easily proven from the teachings of Jesus and the words of Scripture themselves. The whole history of Christian theology illustrates this point. The evidence brought in favor of some point of view—whether a doctrine of the Trinity, or of incarnation, or of the Eucharist, or of whatever sort—can just as often be interpreted equally well in

19. Harnack, *What is Christianity?*, 180.

keeping with a different opinion. Each side has its own reading of the other side's prooftexts. It is very difficult to establish a theological opinion beyond any reasonable doubt merely by appeal to the textual evidence alone. Some people therefore conclude that one needs some further way of establishing in a definitive and binding way what is and is not essential to Christian faith.

That is why many people will often point to the purported authority of the persons that are associated with an opinion in order to "break" the exegetical "tie." Vincent of Lérins famously did exactly this. He wrote that it was necessary to appeal to "the standard of ecclesiastical and catholic interpretation" in order to be able to overcome the "depth" of Scripture which makes it "capable of as many interpretations as there are interpreters" (*Commonitorium* 5). This "standard of ecclesiastical and catholic interpretation" effectively involves an appeal to a purportedly "unanimous" opinion as filtered through the teachings and statements of the "holy ancestors and fathers" and "all or at least almost all priests and doctors" (6). Vincent's reasoning is thus very clear. It may not be possible to prove on the basis of the text alone that this or that interpretation of the Bible is correct, since every heretic throughout history was able to justify his perspective by appeal to Scripture. But at the very least one opinion has "official" approval in the way that another does not, and this "official" approval serves to overcome the difficulty of proving one point of view as truer and more adequate to Scripture than the others on the basis of Scripture alone.

Dahm likewise illustrates this dialectic in his retelling of his conversion to Roman Catholicism. He admits that the orthodoxy of the catholic creeds is not easy to come by on the basis of the scriptural teaching alone. He is then presented with a dilemma:

> What is essential to our faith? Something must be, but this most important question is left without a clear answer if we are without an extrabiblical regula fidei. So I was faced with a dilemma: either I give up the normativity of the creeds for faith, or I give up sola scriptura. I never really considered abandoning the creeds a live option—I did not want a choose-your-own-adventure theology. Sticking with the creeds showed me that I already trusted the Church.[20]

Dahm thus presents the same line of reasoning as Vincent. And this conception of what faith means is very closely related to the notions of "traditionalism" and "hierarchy." The true faith is effectively the authoritative teaching of the hierarchy of the church. But there are many problems with these ideas, the greatest of all being that Jesus himself did not accept them.

20. Dahm, "That Great Revolution of Mind," 101–2.

It has already been argued at some length that there is no basis for the notions of "traditionalism" and "hierarchy" in Jesus's teachings. He rather rejected them. Jesus did not accept that the teachings of certain prominent or important human figures of the past simply as such could be used as "tools" for exercising theological authority. For example, he did not ritually wash his hands before eating just because that was the "tradition of the elders." He also distinguished between human words and the divine word. He did not consider the possibility of a "blending" of the two whether by appeal to human "finality" or "dual agency," so that the fact that a tradition has arisen and gained the endorsement of human authorities does not entail that it comes from God. And Jesus considered that what he says must be believed because it is true (John 8:40), whereas what his apostles say must be believed because they manage successfully to relate and bear witness to what he has said (Matt 28:18–20). The guiding principle is therefore not authority but truth, and truth is independent of authority. The consequence of this is that the line of reasoning proposed by Vincent is foreign to Jesus's way of thinking about these things.

Vincent's argumentation entails that the essential contours of the faith must be defined with reference to the concerns of past generations. This is to say that he is a "traditionalist." These "holy fathers and ancestors" naturally wrote about what seemed important to them in their time. But there is no guarantee that what they considered to be important is actually essential to the faith! After all, Jesus never made any promise to the effect that the prominent teachers of later generations of the church would be providentially guided in their concerns and interpretations. Perhaps then these "holy fathers and ancestors" had preoccupations that Jesus himself did not share; perhaps they had concerns for which Jesus did not actually intend to provide an answer. This matter can only be determined by turning beyond their opinions to the teachings of Jesus himself. Put another way: one must learn from Jesus himself what he cared about so that one knows what to care about as one of his followers. And the rejection of "traditionalism" on Jesus's part means that there is no more necessity in sharing the preoccupations of these "holy fathers and ancestors" to which Vincent refers than there was for Jesus in observing the tradition of ritual handwashing of the "elders" of the Pharisees. Jesus's idea is rather that only the commandment of God come from God's own mouth (so to speak) can unconditionally determine human priorities.

Vincent's way of reasoning is also sophistic. One's rank within a "hierarchical" body is logically irrelevant to the truth of what one says. For example, Jesus did not agree with the "elders" of the Pharisees that one must ritually wash one's hands before eating. These "elders" had rank and esteem but not truth. So also, there have always been bishops in the church who ended up on the "losing" side of every theological controversy throughout history. They too had the episcopate but not the truth. Rank within a "hierarchy" and truth are thus independent of one another; the one does not entail the other. From this it follows that it is a manipulation and a sophism to point out another's inability to prove the truth of his or her own opinions definitively, only later to offer a solution for this inability by appealing to logically irrelevant considerations pertaining to authority within some "hierarchy." This is a matter of noting another's need in some issue and winning his or her submission and loyalty by offering something else altogether that does not actually solve the problem.

One can therefore suggest on the basis of these arguments that the nature of the faith itself must be understood differently. Perhaps this objection presupposes a conception of the faith that is contentious, questionable, and ought to be rejected. But what is Christian faith if one rejects "traditionalism" and "hierarchy"?

Briefly stated, faith is not submission to the authorized dogmas of particular ecclesial authorities, nor can it be defined as belief in this or that very specific and hard to prove doctrine, neither is it adherence to this or that particular tradition that emerges in time within the history of the church. Faith must be understood differently, specifically as a personal commitment to Jesus. To be a Christian is to strive to submit to Jesus's teaching and direction. It is to be committed to him as a student and to entrust one's life and oneself to him; it is an orientation of the heart toward him—allegiance.[21] Karl Barth defines it as follows: "Faith is the orientation of man on Jesus Christ. It is faith in him. The man who believes looks to him, holds to him, and depends on him."[22] And Zwingli: "True piety demands, therefore, that one should hang upon the lips of the Lord and not hear or accept the word of any but the bridegroom."[23] Being a Christian is therefore a personal commitment to Jesus as his student and follower. What is "essential to the faith" is not a particular doctrine or idea but rather an attitude of the heart toward the person Jesus: a willingness and desire to learn from him.

THE NATURE OF THE CHURCH

Christian faith in an individual person is consequently this kind of personal orientation of the heart toward Jesus. But then what is the church? It clearly

21. See Bates, *Salvation by Allegiance Alone.*

22. Barth, *Church Dogmatics* (*CD* hereafter) 4/1:743.

23. Zwingli, *Commentary on True and False Religion*, 92.

must be the sort of community for which the principle of unity is just such a personal orientation. It is akin to an army or band. This metaphor is proposed for example by 1 Clem. 37: "So let us serve as soldiers, brothers, with all seriousness under [Jesus's] orders."[24] One could also say that it is akin to a philosophical school. This means that what makes the church as army to be "one" is the shared loyalty of each member to one and the same leader, just as what makes the church as a school to be "one" is the shared loyalty of each student to Jesus the Teacher.

Every person in the church naturally expresses this faith, commitment, and allegiance differently, because not every person understands Jesus in exactly the same way. A person can only express commitment to Jesus such as he or she understands him, so that each person has to strive to grasp his teachings as well as he or she can. But what makes a person a Christian is not a matter of whether he or she succeeds in understanding Jesus's teachings in this or that way. For example, the soldiers in an army need not agree with one another on everything in order to be a part of one and the same army; all that is required is loyalty to the same general. Neither do students in a school need to agree with one another in order to be a part of one and the same school. So also in the case of the church. To be a Christian is not first and foremost a matter of what a person believes about Jesus but rather of whether a person believes in Jesus. Christian faith is a matter of being oriented toward him in trust, faithfulness, and commitment, regardless of the particular form this orientation takes.

This definition of the church clarifies an important point about the implications of the thesis being argued here. Specifically, it does not entail any such idea as that the church or the gospel "disappeared" or "died" at some point in its history. Christians have always called upon people to entrust themselves to Jesus and to commit to learning from him. There has always been a church as long as there have been people who respond to the preaching about Jesus by entrusting themselves to him. Christ's army has always been on earth; his school has always had students. It is therefore this orientation of the heart and entrusting of oneself to Jesus that makes one to be a part of the one church rather than one's particular theological convictions.

This conception of faith also makes it possible to respond to an argument for the infallibility of the church's magisterium. Francis Sullivan suggests that the church's indefectibility implies that it cannot bind itself to a false or erroneous doctrine, since otherwise its faith would have fallen and the church could not be indefectible anymore. The gates of Hades would have prevailed against it (cf. Matt 16:18). From this it would follow that the

24. In Holmes, *Apostolic Fathers*.

official and binding statements of its magisterium cannot be false.[25] Ludwig Ott also makes such an argument.[26] The idea is thus clear. The indefectibility of the church together with a notion of its life being tied up with its doctrinal commitments entails that its binding declarations cannot be erroneous. What then can be said by way of response?

The first problem with this argument is that it assumes that the faith by which the church lives is first and foremost a matter of believing this or that specific and difficult to prove doctrine in a committed way. The second problem is that it also assumes that the church can in principle bind itself to some doctrine in the way imagined by "traditionalism." This total conception of things is being rejected here.

In the first place, faith in Jesus is an orientation of the heart that is more fundamental than any well-defined theological opinion about him (beyond say the opinion that he alone can be one's teacher and savior). The life of the church is thus its commitment to and love for Jesus. Peter Kreeft writes: "Some popes were positively wicked, but even wicked popes never changed the doctrine. . . . Not a single heresy, not a single compromise of doctrine, no matter how insincere and wicked the teachers were."[27] Whether or not the doctrine of the Roman Catholic Church has always been the same is true is of course an eminently debatable point, unless one circularly admits only a certain category of "official" statements as part of the evidence to consider. Neither can it simply be taken for granted that the magisterial statements of the Roman Catholic Church throughout all time are simply to be taken for granted as true. But the point is irrelevant in any case. A mere change in doctrine would not be the life or death of the church. The church is the church because it wants to sit at Jesus's feet and learn from him, and this dimension can in principle remain unaffected even if some subgroup of Christians come for a time to commit themselves "officially" to false ideas. This church lives when it strives to be obedient to Jesus's teachings, and it dies when it no longer does this, even if it all agrees in some statement of faith.

In the second place, it is also worth noting that "the church" as a whole has never officially bound itself to a doctrine because the church as a whole has always included persons who do not recognize one another's authority or opinions. No one in the church possesses any theological authority beyond the derivative authority of fallibly and in principle reversibly relating and bearing witness to the teachings of Jesus and the works of God in him; no one has the authority to "bind" the whole church

25. Sullivan, *Magisterium*, 16.

26. Ott, *Fundamentals of Catholic Dogma*, 287.

27. Kreeft, "Why?," 131.

except God and Jesus, and there is no binding where they have not spoken on their own. Jesus rejected both "traditionalism" and "hierarchy" in the church, so that a person is not excluded from the church simply because he or she does not follow some particular Christians in illegitimately binding themselves to a contentious doctrine.

This is not to say that there are no right and wrong answers in theology. But what makes for a right or wrong answer? Aristotle defined "truth" as thinking or speaking about things as they are: saying of what is that it is and of what is not that it is not (*Metaphysics* 1011b25). Things are what they are independently of what people think or say about them. Truth is therefore achieved when one's thinking or speaking about a thing is adequate to that thing itself. This is also the perspective assumed here. There is always a truth of the matter in addition to the diversity of opinions that one might encounter among Christians. Some opinions may be wrong while others are right. Now, these differences of opinion can either be ignored or else debated and discussed, depending on one's interests. One should certainly insist that they be debated in a manner that is properly rational and scientific. The goal should be to get at what is true and not necessarily to justify one's prior convictions or the traditions one has come to inherit from others. The goal should be to think and speak truly, and this means thinking or speaking about things such as they are and not necessarily as this or that tradition or community dictates that one think or speak about them. But what makes a person a Christian is that he or she submits to Jesus's claim to authority and wants to understand him better, and one can do this even while coming to a different conclusion than someone else as to what Jesus means to teach on this or that matter.

Being a student obviously does not mean understanding the teacher in the same way as everyone else; it is rather a matter of wanting to understand the teacher such as he or she means to be understood. Being a soldier does not mean being as good a fighter as everyone else; it is rather a matter of wanting to fight as well as one can for one's captain. These same things can be said about being a Christian: it is a matter of wanting properly to understand Jesus so as to obey him. It is of course not simply a matter of appropriating Jesus's words for one's own purpose. A student is not someone who tries to twist the teacher's words in such a way as to justify his or her own opinion. That is not learning but rather appropriating. Neither is one a soldier who interprets the commands in such a way as to conform to one's preferences. Being a Christian, understood as being a student and soldier of Jesus, thus means wanting to know what Jesus means to say and then to do it. This certainly means believing that Jesus is such a good teacher that one ought to commit to him in this way, but this is once more perfectly compatible with misunderstanding Jesus as well as with understanding him differently than others. The personal commitment to Jesus is more fundamental.

The differences in understanding controverted and difficult issues among Christians from throughout history were and remain matters of debate. Each person was able to propose this or that argument in favor of understanding Jesus in this or that way. But each person involved in these disputes was also a student wanting to learn from Jesus; each was wanting to understand what Jesus was proposing and not merely to appropriate Jesus's words for the sake of justifying his own opinions. This means that the theological controversies, discussions, and debates that have taken place in history were thus discussions among equal Christians. Persons on both sides of whatever issue were students of the Messiah who wished to be faithful to what he teaches; they were not discussions taking place between Christians and non-Christians.

CHRISTIAN FAITH AND SALVATION ANXIETY

The question about determining the "essentials" of the faith also seems to have a dimension of "salvation anxiety" to it. Why should a person be so concerned about what is "essential" as a part of the faith that he or she goes looking for infallible ecclesial authorities that Jesus never mentioned? Perhaps it is because he or she is convinced that believing "the wrong things" or failing to believe "the right things" will lead to damnation. Dahm even proposes that there must be an extra-scriptural *regula fidei* because of the ever-present danger of heresy: "Not every Christian, in fact very few Christians, are capable of avoiding heresy on their own through careful study of Scripture. Imagine reading the New Testament as a first-century Jew or pagan. Which of us would realize the creeds?"[28] Yet this fear has no basis in the teachings of Jesus.

Jesus does not teach that a person must believe this or that obscure notion about him to be saved. Harnack put the point well: "How great a departure from what [Jesus] thought and enjoined is involved in putting a 'Christological' creed in the forefront of the Gospel, and in teaching that before a man can approach it he must learn to think rightly about Christ."[29] Jesus preaches the coming of the kingdom of heaven and teaches that one should believe in him and follow him (Mark 1:14–15). Even the demons know that he is "the holy one of God" (v. 24), but presumably this will still not save them. Jesus comes to preach the good news of the kingdom of

28. Dahm, "That Great Revolution of Mind," 100.
29. Harnack, *What is Christianity?*, 147.

heaven; indeed, Jesus teaches what makes it possible for people to enjoy the life of this kingdom. What Jesus wants from a person is thus that he or she commit to him and to come to him in trust. This is plainly and primarily not a matter of believing this or that controverted metaphysical idea about Jesus, but rather of believing in Jesus himself, i.e. of trusting in him. It is not even first a matter of being a particularly good student of his but rather of wanting to be his student, and to all such persons he makes the following promise: "Anyone who comes to me I will never drive away" (John 6:37).

Does it follow from this line of reasoning that "heretics" are also Christians and saved simply because they believe in Jesus? They certainly could be. Why shouldn't one say so? Such persons may admittedly have mistaken ideas about how they are saved, but from this it does not follow that they are not Christians or cannot be saved. Consider the following analogy. A person may not have the right idea about what water is or why it is hydrating, yet water is no less hydrating for that person than for anyone else. So also, salvation is an effect which Jesus produces in a person. It is a matter of his or her enjoying the life of the kingdom of heaven even now, a matter of living in reconciled friendship with God and with other people. Salvation is when a Zacchaeus gives half of his possessions to the poor and repays four times over those whom he has defrauded (Luke 19:1–10). And it is also a matter of Jesus raising that person from the dead and welcoming him into his kingdom. This is what salvation consists in and what every Christian hopes for. And what Jesus wants, once more, is that persons believe in him. He promises that everyone who believes in him will be raised on the last day (John 6:40). There is consequently no obvious reason why he should turn away those who believe in him and have entrusted themselves and their lives to him even while falsely believing various things about him.

It would be one thing if a person were to adhere to a heresy under false pretense or out of a perverse and contrarian desire to undermine what he or she understands to be the true teaching of Jesus. This would be a matter of adopting a theology one knows to be false out of a heart that is rebellious against him. But it is another thing for a person honestly, genuinely, but mistakenly to believe that some heretical variety of Christian faith is the true one. In this latter case a person would sooner be committed to Jesus than to his or her (possibly false) ideas about him. Any such person would be willing in principle to abandon his or her false beliefs about Jesus if they could be shown to be contrary to the truth, and it seems clear that anyone in this latter category would truly believe in Jesus even while believing honestly but wrongly about him. Indeed, heretics have laid their life down for Jesus just as much as the orthodox. These persons went to death for Jesus such as they honestly understood him and in the expectation that

he would save them. Why then should Jesus not accept them? Jesus wishes
to gather up Jerusalem under his wings like a hen would gather her brood
(Matt 23:37). He says these very things about the Pharisees and scribes who
rejected him and whom he called children of Gehenna. Why then should he
turn away the person who does trust in him even while falsely believing this
or that about him? This is not say that such a person will remain a heretic
for the remainder of his or her existence. Presumably the truth comes to
light at some point. But this sort of thing will be true for all persons. It is not
unreasonable to suppose that all persons are in for a theological surprise of
some kind upon death.

Heretics certainly act contrary to Jesus's purposes in their unwitting
rejection of his true teachings, but honesty demands that one admit that
every Christian should hope that Jesus will not count his or her mistakes
and inadvertent opposition to him. Christians are divided on many issues,
and every Christian today must reckon with the real possibility of having
spent his or her life acting contrary to Jesus's true purposes in some important matter or other, especially since even to remain neutral in matters of
controversy is to take a stance that could be mistaken. Therefore no one is
excluded from danger. And Paul speaks thus about those who build on the
foundation of Christ with wood, hay, and straw: "If the work is burned up,
the builder will suffer loss; the builder will be saved, but only as through
fire" (1 Cor 3:15). Why then should this not possibly count in the case of
heretics who taught love for and faith in Jesus but were even radically, profoundly mistaken about this or that dimension of his teaching?

There is a point to be made here. Consider that a person is not made
worthy of Jesus's acceptance because of his or her moral qualities. Salvation
is by grace. Every honest person recognizes in the face of death and the
prospect of *nihil* that salvation at bottom must be a matter of the kindness
of Jesus. This is because nearly everyone who is honest recognizes that there
is very little to say in his or her own favor. Therefore Simon: "We believe that
we will be saved through the grace of the Lord Jesus" (Acts 15:11). It thus
seems consistent with this to say that salvation must be a matter of grace in
the question of one's doctrinal beliefs as well. Some of the heresies which
have been propounded throughout the history of the church are admittedly
an insult to Jesus, but "on that day" every Christian will have to reckon with
the fact that he or she may have often insulted Jesus in some way or another.
Even Paul writes: "I am not aware of anything against myself, but I am not
thereby acquitted. It is the Lord who judges me" (1 Cor 4:4). Every person
should therefore take seriously the possibility that what is acceptable today
may be considered heretical tomorrow (as has frequently been the case).
David Bentley Hart writes: "All too often in Christian history, the word

'heretic' has been just another word for someone who, honestly seeking first the Kingdom of God and its righteousness, has had the misfortune of doing so in a way ultimately pronounced defective either by his contemporaries or (more contemptibly) by later generations."[30] Tomorrow's church can make a heresy of anyone's views. Every person as a matter of necessity must therefore be more fundamentally committed to Jesus himself than to his or her own interpretations of Jesus's teachings.

What is being suggested here is that salvation must be thought a matter of Jesus's kindness, not only in the light of what one has done wrong but also in the light of where one has thought wrongly. Neither should the grave wrongs done by so many prominent Christians throughout history be ignored simply because they believed correctly. It is for whatever reason easier at times to think that Jesus will accept the beloved orthodox of past generations in spite of their serious moral failings—whether it be slavery or political scheming or violence or whatever—than that he will accept the heretical despite their doctrinal failings. Moral failings are "to be expected" as a matter of historical contingency, while doctrinal failings are somehow unforgivable. But there is no obvious reason for making this differentiation apart from bias. Perhaps persons who take pride in their orthodoxy are insulted by the notion that they might equally inherit salvation with heretics. But this seems to be exactly the attitude expressed by those in the parable who had labored all day: they are insulted that the Master in his goodness should be generous to those who (in their judgment) don't deserve it (Matt 20:1–16). One therefore must not turn orthodoxy into a "merit" and a point of spiritual pride any more than one should point to one's various virtues and moral accomplishments.

The heart of Christian faith is not believing controverted things about Jesus but rather clinging to him in one's heart and believing in him despite oneself. It is not essentially a matter of assenting to some complex system of doctrine but rather of committing to Jesus as to one's only hope, indeed of being more committed to Jesus himself than to one's theological opinions. As Thomas Torrance writes: "The stress here is upon the objectivity of grace, not upon faith itself, for in faith we look to Christ and away from ourselves and our own believing. . . . It is Christ who holds on to us and saves us even when our faith is so weak."[31] Faith is a matter of looking away from oneself and toward Christ, just as a chick does not look at itself when clinging to its mother hen. And this should apply as much in matters of doctrinal controversy as in one's own moral merits. It is true that many in

30. Hart, *Tradition and Apocalypse*, 169.
31. Torrance, *Scottish Theology*, 58.

previous generations of the church did not share this way of thinking about the issue of heresy, but then again Christians today are not beholden to all the thoughts and convictions of earlier generations. One may accept the theological conclusions of previous generations of Christians without sharing their attitudes toward those who disagree.

PROTESTANTISM AND CHRISTIAN UNITY

It should be clear at this point that the present work is proposing a different paradigm for understanding the Christian faith than might be thought common or familiar. It may therefore be useful to draw from the points made thus far in order to respond at some length to a common objection brought against Protestantism by Roman Catholic writers, theologians, and philosophers. This is the claim that Protestantism cannot accomplish unity in the church. The denial of an authoritative ecclesial institution leads to what philosopher Neal Judisch calls "hermeneutical chaos and ecclesial anarchy."[32] White likewise speaks of the "splintering of doctrinal divisions" afflicting Protestantism.[33] Responding to this objection by drawing from the various notions presented above should help to make clear the paradigm of thought of the present work. How then to respond?

It may be possible to turn this argumentation around. Perhaps the blame does not lie with Protestantism so much as with the catholic or mainstream theological tradition out of which it emerged, more specifically with what this mainstream tradition wants, with its theoretical preoccupations, and with its presupposed conception of what constitutes "unity." One can even suggest that the vision being proposed in the present essay can do a better job of identifying the true nature of Christian unity beyond the diversity of theological opinions. It may be that a genuine unity can be found when one gives up both the catholic conception of "faith" as well as the specific speculative-metaphysical concerns of the catholic tradition in favor of the actual teachings of Jesus. Faith should no longer be thought of as a conviction about this or that controverted issue but rather a personal commitment to Jesus as one's teacher, and the Christian life should be understood not as a matter of metaphysical speculation but rather of the practical enactment of his clear teachings regarding what it means to live here and now as a child of God in the kingdom of heaven. These points can be explained and argued as follows.

32. Judisch, "Of Towers and Tongues," 108n27.
33. White, *Light of Christ*, 186.

The predominant mentality for a long time in the church catholic was that theological controversies need to be resolved in a definitive way. One needed to have a firm opinion on any issue that people cared enough about to debate. There had to be a definite answer to the question of whether Jesus was consubstantial with the Father, or of whether anyone would go to hell forever, or whether Christ had two wills or only one will, or whether it is appropriate to fashion and venerate images in the churches, or of whether and how the bread and wine of the eucharistic meal really do become the body and blood of Jesus, or of whether Mary was conceived without original sin and taken away to heaven at the end of her life. But there is much to say against this mentality. The truth is that the majority of these issues can hardly be established to everyone's satisfaction on the basis of the available evidence. Anyone who is honest recognizes this fact. Each one of these issues has been and remains a subject of continual debate. This is because they are debates about speculative metaphysical matters. They are "metaphysical" in that they are not debates about things that are apparent in the world of experience, and there is no resolving them by simply attending to experience in the way that Jesus could show the wounds in his hands and side to his disciples after the resurrection. And the serious student of theology knows that every position one can take on these matters is subject to considerable counter-arguments and objections from others. This is true not only of the various positions themselves but also of the entailments and presuppositions of each position. No one can claim to be beyond objection or problem.

The doctrine of the Trinity provides a fine example of this. The *Quicunque Vult* (or "Athanasian Creed") teaches that one has no chance of salvation if one does not hold firmly to such statements of faith as this: "So the Father is God, the Son is God, and the Holy Ghost is God. And yet they are not three Gods, but one God."[34] Dale Tuggy thinks to the contrary that the doctrine of the Trinity is hopelessly confused and contradictory and that the Bible teaches a unitarian conception of God.[35] Lewis Ayres thinks that the doctrine of the Trinity must be understood in light of the classical doctrine of divine simplicity.[36] R. T. Mullins thinks that the doctrine of divine simplicity as well as other theological commitments of "classical theism" ultimately undermine the coherence of distinctly Christian doctrines.[37] Richard Plantinga, Thomas Thompson, and Matthew Lundberg think that the doctrine of divine simplicity leads to an objectionable conception of

34. In Schaff, *Creeds of Christendom*, 2:66–71.
35. Tuggy, "Metaphysics and the Logic of the Trinity."
36. Ayres, *Nicaea and Its Legacy*.
37. Mullins, *End of the Timeless God*.

God's providential relation to the world.[38] They therefore adopt a "social" conception of the Trinity following Jürgen Moltmann.[39] Brian Leftow thinks "social" trinitarianism compromises the Christian commitment to monotheism as well as the notions of divine omnipotence and omniscience.[40] R. P. C. Hanson writes that the non- and pro-Nicene parties alike approached the biblical texts with presuppositions that can only seem naïve and inappropriate to readers trained in modern hermeneutics.[41] Thomas McCall thinks there is a better case for social trinitarianism of a sort in the Bible than for the alternatives.[42] Karl Barth insists against the "social" model that the "persons" or *hypostaseis* of the Trinity are certainly not each a distinct "I" or conscious self.[43] Oliver Crisp thinks that the dogma of the Trinity is at best a kind of "theological inference to the best explanation" from the data of Scripture and early testimony to the apostolic message and that every extant model of the Trinity tries to say too much about it.[44] And Karl Rahner thinks that the doctrine is "an absolute mystery that we do not understand even after it has been revealed."[45]

These sorts of debates can thus go on *ad nauseam*. The point here is obviously not to deny the doctrine of the Trinity—although the brief discussion above seems to show that there may not be any one such thing as "the" doctrine of the Trinity beyond perhaps a certain approved way of speaking. The point is rather to invite honesty about the actual state of things in theology. Every response to an objection raises new objections and new possible counter-responses. The Proverb remains true: "The one who first states a case seems right, until the other comes and cross-examines" (Prov 18:17). This is the way of things in theology because it is way of things in all of human life. Things are ambiguous and multiply interpretable; these are conditions that characterize the human experience of the world simply as such.

Dahm writes that he could not take seriously the option of giving up the unconditional normativity of the orthodox creeds and the corresponding notion of an ecclesial magisterium: "I did not want a

---

38. Plantinga et al., *Introduction to Christian Theology*.

39. Moltmann, *Trinity and the Kingdom*.

40. Leftow, "Anti Social Trinitarianism."

41. Hanson, *Search for the Christian Doctrine of God*, 848–49.

42. McCall, *Which Trinity? Whose Monotheism?*, 87–89; McCall, *Analytic Christology*, 165–75.

43. Barth, *CD* 1/1:351–60.

44. Crisp, *Analyzing Doctrine*, 85, 82.

45. Rahner, *Trinity*, 50.

choose-your-own-adventure theology."[46] Here he gives an example of what Harnack had called "the old and almost ineradicable tendency of mankind to rid itself of its freedom and responsibility in higher things and subject itself to a law. . . . It is much easier, in fact, to resign oneself to any, even the sternest, kind of authority, than to live in the liberty of the good."[47] But there is no escaping the conditions of fallibility which inevitably make all of human life in every respect a "choose-your-own-adventure." Every choice a person makes is founded upon a fallible grasp of things. People see things only as well as their sense of sight allows, read only as well as their reading knowledge of a language allows, understand theological realities only as well as their prior commitments and ways of thinking about things allow them. One does not simply experience the world straightaway but always also oneself to some extent; there is subjectivity in every presumed objectivity, and one cannot escape oneself to see things just as they are. This means that one is always having to make a choice about how to respond to things such as one can appreciate them, yet without the certainty that one is seeing things aright. And all this is as equally true of ecclesial hierarchs as of ordinary mortals. The desire for a centralized theological authority capable of giving a definitive answer and an end to the "hermeneutical chaos" is a fantasy. There is no such thing. The introduction of one more participant of whatever pretended authority into any theological dispute does not overcome all subjectivity but merely adds a further subjectivity into the mix.

Consider that there is no "infallible magisterium" in science. Scientists disagree with one another about their theories and about the interpretation of the data. Some of these disagreements are quite significant, being consequential for human life on earth, and yet there is no centralized authority structure that can intervene in these debates to make infallible pronouncements about which of many competing scientific theories is the correct one. But no one thinks to posit that there be such a thing! And it is also obvious that instituting such a body would not actually solve any scientific debates. People are not infallible simply because they say they are. Proposing such a magisterium would accomplish no more than the addition of one further opinion into a debate. Yet so many persons are convinced that the presence of such a body in matters of theology would in fact resolve disputes. Why should this be?

One might think that this is because most people (implicitly or not) think of the Christian faith as a matter of submission to authority. It is not about submitting to an idea because one sees for oneself that it is true or at

---

46. Dahm, "That Great Revolution of Mind," 101.

47. Harnack, *What is Christianity?*, 118–19.

least believable. One submits rather because it is propounded by a person whose authority one accepts ahead of time for whatever reason. Perhaps one also submits because of a threat associated with the refusal to submit. Such persons consequently think that adherence to the dogmas of the church is a positive act demanded by Jesus, and failure to perform this positive act would be a disobedience that demands a punishment. Thus, disputes about the interpretation of the proposals of these authorities could be resolved by simply positing the continuing presence of the relevant sort of authorities to the present day. Theology becomes fundamentally a matter of appealing to authority rather than of purely rational argumentation, as Henry Chadwick would characterize the difference between Berengarius and Lanfranc of Bec in the Middle Ages.[48] Disobedience to these authorities is punished with excommunication and the threat of damnation. Belief is ultimately founded on authority.

This is precisely the mentality that has been combatted in this text. It is entirely mistaken and foreign to Jesus's thinking. Appeals to "tradition" and "hierarchy" are not "tools" for exercising theological authority in his messianic community. There is no infallible hierarchy of the church because Jesus never spoke about or promised any such thing. He sent his disciples into the world to teach all people to obey the things he taught them (Matt 28:20). Even the apostles themselves did not present themselves as religious authorities to be believed because of their position within a "hierarchy." They presented themselves as persons relating and bearing witness to something they experienced for themselves: "What we have heard, what we have seen with our eyes, what we have looked at and touched with our hands" (1 John 1:1). This entire "authoritarian" approach to the question of belief thus has no basis in Jesus's words or in the self-conception of the apostles. They did not argue by appeal to their position of authority within a "hierarchy." It is only later hierarchs who appear later in the history of the church that make such appeals, perhaps in order to motivate submission to their opinions apart from any convincing proof of their truth.

There is also the inconvenient fact that most of the controversies debated in the history of theology had to do with issues on which Jesus touched very little if at all. What did Jesus ever say about whether or not his mother was a perpetual virgin or conceived without original sin or assumed into heaven? What did he ever say about the fabrication and veneration of images in the church? When did he ever clearly and unambiguously discourse about the precise ontological relation between the two natures? When did he ever clarify whether he possessed two wills or one? When did he ever

48. Cf. Chadwick, "Ego Berengarius," 427.

specify that he possesses a human rational soul in addition to a body? Most of these theological disputes seem profoundly alien to the concerns that Jesus had while preaching and teaching during his time on earth. Jesus never affirms precisely what some later official opinion will affirm in exactly the same words. These opinions sometimes have at best a slim connection to certain incidental remarks of his, and later generations of Christians with their own historically contingent concerns and preoccupations came to find something suggestive in what he says on these occasions. But the words Jesus actually uses generally can mean one thing when received in one theoretical context and something else when received in another. "I am he" (John 8:24) could be an (indirect) affirmation of Christ's consubstantiality with the Father according to pro-Nicene theologians, while to non-Nicenes it is an assertion of Jesus's status as Messiah. One might therefore wonder with Hart whether official dogmas are not sooner products of the historical and social contexts in which they arose than of the actual teachings of Jesus himself.[49] They could well be unprovable speculations that make use of Jesus's words for purposes foreign to his own intentions and interests. Dahm himself seems to fall into this conclusion when he writes: "Not every Christian, in fact very few Christians, are capable of avoiding heresy on their own through careful study of Scripture. Imagine reading the New Testament as a first-century Jew or pagan. Which of us would realize the creeds?"[50] This is effectively an admission that the later orthodoxy is not (plainly, demonstrably) native to the New Testament. Jesus taught people how to relate to God and to one another so as to open up the kingdom of heaven, but later ecclesial figures wanted to speculate about questions of metaphysics and the unknowable distant past or future.

Yet none of this apparently mattered for a very long time in the history of the church catholic. A controversy and a debate had arisen; Christians could not get along; they began to condemn each other to hell; it thus had to be ended by someone or other; it had to come down in favor of some particular opinion. This mentality then led to the novelty of ecumenical councils and other such purportedly authoritative interventions on the part of the magisterium of the historical church.

Where then did Protestantism come from? It arose in time because the answers that had been reached by past generations of the church were no longer convincing to everyone. They raised more problems than they had solved; they did not seem to square with what was written in the Bible or with what seemed rational. And yet Protestants at the same time inherited

49. See the discussion in Hart, *Tradition and Apocalypse*.
50. Dahm, "That Great Revolution of Mind," 100.

from their catholic predecessors this same mentality preoccupied with having a definite answer to certain ambiguous and difficult questions. They shared this generally catholic notion of Christian faith as centrally preoccupied with speculative matters of debate. It is just that now a variety of answers to these disputed questions were being proposed among them, and it was also newly possible in the Reformation to hold to an opinion and to propagate it far and wide without necessarily opening oneself up to the threat of being excluded from the only available church or even of being killed for one's convictions. The world in general seemed to be open to new ideas. The diversity of Protestant theologies thus arose in new and different social conditions of such a nature as to permit their survival and even flourishing over time.

Why did these diverse theologies become distinct "churches"? Why did they not have the same institutional unity that the Roman Catholic Church had? The answer is clear: because of the mentality and conception of the faith inherited from the very catholic tradition from which they emerged. Many of the early Protestants were not happy to stick as much as possible to teachings of Jesus and to allow everything that goes beyond them to be a matter of opinion and an academic curiosity. This was not how they understood Christian faith. They needed firm and "official" answers to disputed questions about matters in which a clear and definitive answer is not possible. Harnack writes: "From the year 1526 onwards national Churches had to be founded at headlong speed on evangelical lines; they were forced to be 'rounded and complete' at a time when much was still in a state of flux."[51] This is the way of thinking they inherited from the mainstream theological tradition, and it is why they divided amongst themselves into so many groups: their contingent historical circumstances.

The complaint that Protestantism leads to anarchy is thus unfair. It is true that Protestants did not have the appropriate mentality for dealing with differences, but this does not owe to the fact that they were Protestants. They understandably but regrettably inherited an unfortunate way of thinking from the catholic theological tradition from which they emerged. It would be more accurate to say that it is the catholic notion of faith as a firm conviction about certain speculative, ambiguous, and debatable matters that leads to "anarchy"—specifically so long as it is not complemented by the threat of excommunication or even death at the hand of the civil magistrate working in collaboration with the ecclesial authorities. That is what prevented "anarchy" and the enduring multiplication of churches in the earlier days of the mainstream theological tradition: not the clarity of

51. Harnack, *What is Christianity?*, 289.

the truth but rather the real threat of excommunication or even punishment and death for dissenters.

The Protestants inherited from their theological predecessors the idea that there had to be a definite answer to every theological question they imagined to be important. They consequently began to define themselves precisely in terms of their opinions by which they differed from others. The differences became the markers of their identities. Some of them even inherited the catholic notion that dissidents in matters of belief could rightly be killed for their "heresies." The tendency for "anarchy" thus owes to the catholic notion of the faith. It is the need to have a definite answer to endlessly debatable questions that leads to the divisions—so long as there is not one person or group of persons at the top who can threaten their theological opponents with death. But Jesus did not grant such authority to anyone!

The significance of the thesis of the present work for Protestant theology is therefore clear. There can be no returning to the prejudices and dogmatisms of yesteryear. There is need of a different mentality and different preoccupations. One needs to be willing not to be dogmatic about everything. One needs to be willing to accept that definitive answers cannot be given to every interesting and seemingly important question; some things should be left as a matter of opinion. Most importantly of all, one's theological priorities must be dictated by what Jesus actually addresses, instead of by the things that make one curious. Zwingli once more: "True piety demands, therefore, that one should hang upon the lips of the Lord and not hear or accept the word of any but the bridegroom."[52] There is enough in the actual teachings of Jesus to provide a firm basis for Christian unity, even granting that all the speculative questions with which theology has been preoccupied for so long are relativized as matters of opinion and academic curiosities.

This is not the first time in the history of theology that such an attitude has been proposed. Irenaeus himself appreciated the wisdom in leaving some matters without a final answer. He saw that his gnostic opponents caused trouble in the church by trying to come up with speculative answers to questions without a proper and explicit basis in Jesus's own teachings. They invented these vast speculative systems for which there was effectively little actual evidence.[53] And they caused divisions and problems among Christians because they insisted on these hard-to-prove speculations against contrary opinions. Irenaeus thus writes: "If, therefore, . . . we leave some questions in the hands of God, we shall both preserve our faith uninjured, and shall continue without danger" (*Against Heresies* 2.28.3).

---

52. Zwingli, *Commentary on True and False Religion*, 92.

53. See Marjanen and Luomanen, *Companion to Second-Century Christian "Heretics."*

Irenaeus thought the gnostics and all Christians would do better to be humble and to stick to what is clearly there in the text. This same lesson is also being proposed here.

The mainstream theological tradition understood the Christian faith as a matter of assenting to very specific doctrinal formulas and ideas. The present essay is proposing a different conception of faith that makes it possible to see a deeper Christian unity in the church beyond the diversity of theologies. Consider how the variety of theologians and philosophers mentioned earlier can all be called "trinitarian" in spite of the real diversity in their interpretations of the Nicene-Constantinopolitan faith. Karl Barth, Jürgen Moltmann, and William Hasker are perhaps as far as possible from believing the same things as regards their conceptions of the inner being of God, and yet they are "trinitarian" because they are committed to the Nicene-Constantinopolitan faith apart from their particular interpretations and receptions of it. They are most fundamentally "trinitarian" in virtue of the orientation of allegiance in their heart to this particular creed and the community which emitted it. The same thing is therefore true in the question of Christian faith in general. To be a Christian is not a matter of believing this or that particular doctrine. It is rather a matter of the orientation of one's heart, of sitting in one's heart at the feet of Jesus the Messiah and Teacher of the church and wanting to learn from him. The will of God is that a person believe in the name of his Son and love others (1 John 3:23). And every person who does the will of God is a brother, sister, or mother to Jesus. This is what Jesus had said about the crowds that were gathering around him to hear his teachings (Matt 12:46–50). To be a disciple is therefore to sit at Jesus's feet and listen to him. It is to be committed to him and to try to learn from him as well as one can; it does not necessarily mean coming to particular conclusions about what he means to say.

Theological disputes are all matters of opinion. Christians can certainly cooperate with one another to try to understand what Jesus means to teach. They can use their gifts for each other's benefit. But it is important to realize that these differences of opinion do not make them students of different masters. The diversity of theological opinions does not affect the unity of all Christians in the church. Christians are also certainly free to congregate with like-minded persons who think in roughly the same ways. Some may think this or that way of acting or believing is right while others think otherwise. The ideal is of course that all Christians agree. Yet it might at times be better (as an accommodation to the ubiquitous phenomenon of Christian hard-heartedness) to multiply congregations than to live in constant fighting or bickering. But it must be insisted that Protestants of various kinds, Roman Catholics, and Eastern Orthodox are not any less Christians simply because they see things differently. The church is not "divided" into many just because they are not all in agreement. They are all equally students of one and the same Messiah (Matt 23:10). They all equally entrust themselves and their lives over to him; they all try to be loyal soldiers of one and the same captain. That is what makes them to be Christians and one church: the interior orientation to the person of Jesus. And it is compatible with the diversity of their beliefs and practices. They are not any less "one" as Christians because what makes them to be Christians in the first place is not that by which they are distinguished.

There is thus nothing intrinsically "anarchic" about the sort of Protestantism being proposed in this essay. It has one authority: Jesus and his teachings. It also has one goal: to understand these teachings as well as possible and to live in obedience to them. It is only "anarchic" for the person who believes that everyone must think in exactly the same way (as he or she) about certain controverted and debatable issues. It is anarchic for the person who does not accept diversity of interpretation. But no one is required to accept this notion of what would constitute "unity." After all, everyone admits that some things are best left as matters of opinion. The present work can be understood as arguing that more things ought to be thought of as matters of opinion than many are perhaps accustomed to grant, the boundary line being drawn by the clear teachings of Jesus. It is also true that the perspective of the present essay does not grant to any mere human being the pretense of being able to speak definitively and bindingly about some matter. This is because Jesus himself did not grant anyone any such authority. No one has any further theological authority than that of fallibly and in principle reversibly bearing witness to what Jesus has said and taught. This alone is what he commissioned his disciples to do.

No one other than God can give a final answer to the theological questions that have been debated for ages. Perhaps the truth will remain uncertain until it is revealed eschatologically at the restoration of all things. This was the perspective of the theologian Wolfhart Pannenberg.[54] It seems agreeable and consonant with the facts of human fallibility. This is also a good thing because it means that future generations of Christians have the freedom to correct the errors of past generations if these should become evident in time. One therefore should not presume to speak definitively where Jesus has remained silent. But it is also worth emphasizing the further point that the mere pretense to "finality" or "infallibility" of pronouncement on the part of some person does not mean that the truth has actually been reached. Someone can claim to speak on behalf of God and even to

---

54. See Pannenberg, *Systematic Theology*, ch. 1.

excommunicate or kill those who refuse to submit to his opinions; he may even convince many people to agree with him; he may have the means available to him to enforce his ideas violently in the church. None of this means that they are true!

Zwingli writes that the decrees of the church do not make things true. For example, the virgin Mary is not a virgin simply because the church decrees that she is one. These decrees must rather correspond to facts of the matter which are what they are independently of the decrees themselves: "For unless she were a virgin in her own quality, they could not make her a virgin by their decrees. Her virginity is based on the fact, not on the decrees of men."[55] The church's decrees are thus not magical speech; they cannot make things true but rather must strive to describe things truly. It is true that testimony is often treated in theology as though it were as evidentially valuable as direct perception. "Official" testimony from ecclesial hierarchs is especially so valuable for many. Vincent of Lérins illustrates this mentality. But it is a deception. Speech of any kind is just speech; it does not make true. People can speak falsely because things are what they are apart from what anyone says about them, and there is no basis for thinking that the words of anyone in the church, whether "official" or otherwise, are ever guaranteed to be true. The New Testament rather teaches that persons who are to be called to the position of bishop must antecedently be trustworthy and knowledgeable (1 Tim 3:2; Titus 1:9). This implies that a person could be a bishop and yet be theologically unreliable. Consider how a police officer should be honorable and have respect for the law and for human life. This does not mean that every actual police officer satisfies these criteria! There is consequently no guarantee that "official" ecclesial speech is true. Only the thing itself makes speech about it to be true or false. The only thing that should matter in theology is truth, and truth is not a matter of authority; it is a matter of thinking and talking about things such as they are, independently of what anyone thinks or says about them.

Someone might note that the apostle Paul taught that Christians should seek to "say the same thing" (1 Cor 1:10). It is therefore important that Christians be in agreement with one another. This is true. But there are different ways to achieving such unity in a situation of disagreement about some issue. One way is to insist that everyone agree with one particular opinion being offered in this ongoing dispute on pain of exclusion from the group or even death. This is a matter of accomplishing unity by violent enforcement of a particular opinion. Another way to unity is to set the debate to the side as a curiosity, or to treat it as a speculative academic interest and

55. Zwingli, *Commentary on True and False Religion*, 114.

matter of opinion, and to accord the proper priority to what everyone has in common or to what Jesus himself taught explicitly. This is also a way of "saying the same thing": by refusing to debate or split apart over a contentious matter. It is to allow that actual clear teachings of Jesus to dictate one's priorities. Zwingli argued in precisely this manner:

> If now you find a different teaching in the Fathers than that which is contained in the teaching of Christ and if you abide by that of the Fathers more, it must needs follow that you are not in the church or communion of God but in the church of the Fathers. At that point they retort, "One has to be able to become united through the common voice of the gathered Fathers." Answer: No. One has to be united through the one word of God.[56]

Christians thus should indeed all "say the same thing." But this does not entail that they need to be talking about particular subject matters which in the end bind them to particular "Fathers" or teachers. They should rather be saying the same thing by remaining with the teachings left by Christ, who speaks for himself and who should not be confused with his later followers. And this is evidently what Paul himself did in response to the controversies about teachers at Corinth. He pointed his audience back to Jesus and erased any ultimately meaningful distinction between the teachers in the church at that time.

There is no reason why this option could not have been taken more often in Christian history, nor is there a reason why it could not be taken more often in the present. Consider how the Nicene and non-Nicene theologians disagreed about whether the Father and Son are consubstantial. This is a disagreement about metaphysics. It is not a disagreement that could be resolved by appeal to the way Jesus looked in experience. Neither is it a disagreement about the things Jesus taught about prayer or doing good to others or believing in him or loving God with all one's being. It is a disagreement about some dimension of Jesus's being that is experientially inaccessible, which cannot be perceived but only thought about. It is likewise arguable that the difference between the two views is ultimately inconsequential. For example, Jesus prays in the garden: "Not what I will but what you will" (Matt 26:39). This would seem to suggest that Jesus is not consubstantial with God. There are two wills and thus two beings. By way of response, one could note with Crisp the traditional answer that the "willing" here is done by Jesus in his humanity.[57] He thus still retains his consubstantiality with the Father as regards his divinity. But this implies that the humanity of Jesus possesses an

---

56. Zwingli, "Exposition of the Sixty-Seven Articles," 46.

57. Crisp, *Analyzing Doctrine*, 188.

"I" of its own that is the subject of its own willing. Put another way, Jesus's humanity has self-awareness. There is no such thing as human "willing" that does not belong to a human "I" or conscious subject that is aware of itself as willing this or that. Jesus's own words themselves imply that they are spoken by an "I" that is aware of itself as willing something, identifies itself as the subject of this willing, and submits to the potentially contrary will of God: "Not what I want." That is a human "I" and not a divine "I" speaking. Yet John of Damascus summarizes the classical tradition when he says that there is in God only "one will, one operation, alike in three persons."[58] From this follows Rahner's insistence that there is "only one real consciousness in God" or divine "I."[59] As Barth would write, the *hypostaseis* of the Trinity are not each a distinct "I" or subject of experience.[60] And the impassibility of this divine "I" implies that it is unchanged and unaffected by the things that happen to the humanity of Jesus. Incarnation thus does not mean that human experiences are introduced into the consciousness of the divine "I." Neither does it make any sense for a single "I" be the subject of two wills. Donald Fairbairn correctly maintains that the concern of the Nicene-Chalcedonian perspective is to safeguard the assertion that God himself had "personally" come into the world in Jesus.[61] But what then is the ultimately significant difference between the Nicene and non-Nicene position, or how has God "personally" come into the world, if one grants that the human soul of Jesus is self-aware and thus has an experiential or phenomenological "I" of its own distinct from the divine "I"? What real difference does the hypostatic union make in the end, or what more is it than an imagined justification for a certain preferred way of speaking, if both sides of the debate agree that there is not one phenomenological "I" that is simultaneously the subject of divine and human experiences?[62] These considerations incline one to agree with Harnack's verdict: "In the course of this [Christological] controversy men put an end to brotherly fellowship for the sake of a nuance; and thousands were cast out, condemned, loaded with chains and done to death."[63] But leave this point to the side. These parties could have agreed that Father and Son are functionally inseparable as far as salvation and Christian life is concerned. One cannot have fellowship with the Father without the Son and *vice versa*, neither can one know the Father except through the Son. They

58. John of Damascus, "On Heresies," 161.

59. Rahner, *Trinity*, 107.

60. Barth, *CD* 1/1:351–60; Rahner, *Trinity*, 106–9.

61. Fairbairn, *Grace and Christology*, 22.

62. Cf. Mullins, "Classical Theism, Christology, and the Two Sons Worry."

63. Harnack, *What is Christianity?*, 125; emphasis removed.

could have agreed on the unique mediatorial work of Jesus. This would have been an adequate compromise with far greater explicit support in the actual teachings of Jesus than either ontological alternative. Why then shouldn't this have been the notion defining Christian faith for centuries to come rather than the ontological speculation about consubstantiality?

The Christian theologians of those generations were admittedly metaphysicians. They thought such matters of metaphysics were essential to the faith. That is why they would not have agreed that a statement about the mediatorial work of Jesus would have sufficed; these metaphysical differences mattered to them too much for them. Athanasius for example wrote that one contemplates God "when men's mind has no intercourse with the body, and has nothing of the latter's desires mingled with it from outside but is entirely superior to them, being self–sufficient as it was created in the beginning, . . . [transcending] the senses and all human things and [rising] high above the world" (*Contra Gentes* 2). The contemplation of God is thus metaphysical in the strict sense that it takes place in the realm of pure thought, in the consideration of being in itself, in abstraction from the world of human experience. But there is no compelling reason why the Christians of today must also be metaphysicians concerned about the same things[64]—especially when Jesus's own teachings seem to have little to do with this. Where does Jesus teach anything about contemplating God in abstraction from the senses and rising high above the world? Finding common ground and a shared conception of the faith among those that disagree may require abstaining from contentious metaphysical speculations of this sort, but it would also involve staying closer to the actual teachings of Jesus. And it goes without saying that metaphysical speculation was not left as a "tool" for exercising theological authority in the church.

It is notable also that the New Testament warns about people who are "conceited, knowing nothing, having a morbid craving for controversy and for disputes about words" (1 Tim 6:4). Teachers in the church should instead seek to teach "the sound words of our Lord Jesus Christ and the teaching that accords with godliness" (v. 3). Hence one can understand that there is simply no basis in Scripture for thinking that there must be a way to resolve every possible theological controversy. Not everything that people have disputed about in the history of the church can be definitively settled by appeal to the biblical or rational evidence alone. The only originally authoritative teachings in the church are "the sound words of our Lord Jesus Christ." These are what should be spoken. As Harnack summarizes them: "To know God as one's Father, to possess a God of grace, to find comfort in His grace and

---

64. See Nemes, *Theology of the Manifest*.

providence, to believe in the forgiveness of sins."[65] These alone are the "tools" by which theological authority is exercised; this is what a teacher must concern him- or herself with. It would therefore seem to follow that Jesus himself did not care about everything that was important to others and debated in the history of Christian theology, and this would make it seem entirely out of place for the church to accord to these matters a greater importance than Jesus himself did during his time on earth. The New Testament text offers a warning against precisely this kind of misplaced preoccupation.

It is for some reason especially in the domain of religious faith that admitting the fallibility of human beings and demanding a corresponding restraint in the exercise of theological authority is taken as raising the specter of utter anarchy and chaos. This kind of worry can give one the impression that there is little more than the threat of exclusion or violence or damnation motivating widespread submission to certain theological opinions. Such a thing seems plausible especially in the light of the speculative metaphysical nature of so many purportedly essential doctrines. Yet Jesus did not authorize anyone in his church to impose their convictions on others with threats, and it may well be that many persons tacitly recognize just how flimsy and uncertain a foundation in the actual teachings of Jesus many purportedly "necessary" doctrines actually have.

The suggestion can therefore be made that Christians certainly should all "say the same thing," but they should do this by limiting their strongly held and defining opinions to what Jesus has taught. They should not venture to speculate and to try to force submission to opinions that Jesus himself did not clearly teach; Jesus did not leave them what they are looking for. It is true that past generations of Christians found certain debates to be of central importance, and these include debates about metaphysics. But it does not follow that Christians today must think they are equally important. Consider how it was a tradition of the elders that all Jews ritually wash their hands before eating. These elders thought this issue was important enough to pass on to later generations, and yet Jesus did not think that he and his disciples were beholden to the convictions of the elders who did not have a divine commandment in support of their opinion! This is because past generations can err even while the error does not become evident until later. Neither therefore are Christians of the present day necessarily beholden to the concerns and preoccupations of previous generations except insofar as these can be grounded in a commandment of Jesus. It is Jesus and not his followers who establish Christian priorities.

65. Harnack, *What is Christianity?*, 284.

Someone might wonder: What is left of the faith if the speculative metaphysical concerns of past generations are relativized as matters of opinion? What is the faith if it is not (for example) a firmly held conviction about the nature of justification or the relation between the two natures of Christ? In fact there is still very much left. It is true that renouncing or at least de-emphasizing the speculative metaphysical questions with which the catholic tradition was preoccupied for so long would change the shape of Christian life in certain notable ways. More specifically, retreating from metaphysical speculation to the world of experience naturally means putting a greater emphasis on matters of action, so that Christian faith becomes a principally ethical, spiritual, and practical affair, rather than the contemplation and even dogmatic enforcement of metaphysical speculations. But this would also mean returning to a certain simplicity and practicality more characteristic of the faith in its earliest stages. Pliny the Younger famously described the meetings of Christians to the emperor Trajan around the year 110 CE as follows:

> [T]hey were accustomed to assemble at dawn on a fixed day, to sing a hymn antiphonally to Christ as [to a] God, and to bind themselves by an oath, not for the commission of some crime, but to avoid acts of theft, brigandage, and adultery, not to break their word, and not to withhold money deposited with them when asked for it. When these rites were completed, it was their custom to depart, and then to assemble again to take food, which was however common and harmless (*Letters* 10.96).

The emphasis of these gatherings was ethical, spiritual, and practical. Christians met with each other to worship Jesus together, to promise to one another that they would follow his teachings, and then to celebrate the fact of their salvation and the forgiveness of their sins through Jesus's death and anticipate his eschatological return by the meal of the Eucharist.[66] The early eucharistic prayers prescribed in the Didache for during and after the meal illustrate this very point: "We give you thanks, Holy Father, for your holy name, which you have caused to dwell in our hearts, and for the knowledge and faith and immortality that you have made known to us through Jesus your servant; to you be the glory forever" (Did. 10:2). And: "Just as this broken bread was scattered upon the mountains and then was gathered together and became one, so may your church be gathered together from the ends of the earth into your kingdom" (9:4). Afterwards they returned to living everyday life in the world as children of God and students and followers of Jesus the Messiah.

---

66. Cf. McGowan, *Ancient Christian Worship*, 30–31.

Pliny's retelling, together with the depiction of things in the Didache, paints a picture of the earliest church as an "eschatological Jesus book club and charitable meal society." This is what the church can be in the world when it renounces or at least relativizes the prejudices and preoccupations of its catholic predecessors. Jeremiah Cowart complains that the American evangelicalism he had experienced before becoming Roman Catholic seemed to bear no resemblance to what he presumed to be the ornate liturgy of the Old Testament Hebrews and earliest Christians.[67] But the opinion of the present author is that nothing at all of true substance would be lost by returning to this olden simplicity of the faith: a weekly recapitulation of the teachings of Jesus (perhaps by means of an edifying discourse) and a grateful celebration of the accomplishment of salvation and the hope of a new world through a shared meal. Of course, the precise liturgical form of this celebration clearly does not matter in the end so long as its purpose is met. Harnack once more insisted that "the community assembled for God's worship is to proclaim the message of God with praise and thanksgiving, and call upon His name. Anything that goes beyond that is not worship at all."[68] What more is needed, then?

Christians in the beginning gathered for the sake of reorienting themselves for the week to come on the basis of Jesus's teachings and in remembrance of the fact of their salvation as commemorated through a meal. They conferred with one another as a part of their shared life-project of living in the kingdom of heaven opened up to human beings by Jesus's teachings. They confessed their sins to one another and prayed for one another (Jas 5:16). They also consulted with one another about how best to help others who were in need (cf. 1 John 3:17). They gathered so as to remind one another of how to live as children of God in the world in the days that would follow. They were a society for doing good "for all people and especially for those of the household of faith" (Gal 6:10). They fed the widows and the poor daily (cf. Acts 6:1). Indeed, James said it well: "Religion that is pure and undefiled before God the Father is this: to care for orphans and widows in their distress and to keep oneself unstained by the world" (Jas 1:27). Rich and poor ate at the same table (cf. 1 Cor 11:21–22; Jas 2:2–6). The earliest Christians thus lived as a community of God's children in the world; they lived ordinary human lives as people who were convinced that human beings are the children of God, redeemed from sin and death by the sacrifice of Jesus. These are the things that really matter. This is therefore what a Christianity without speculative-metaphysical preoccupations would like:

67. Cowart, "Crawl, Walk, Run," 79–80.
68. Harnack, *What is Christianity?*, 272.

to a great extent the way the faith looked in the beginning. And it should be further noted that the renunciation of metaphysical speculations—or at least the refusal to turn these speculative and academic curiosities into purportedly "essential" doctrines which distinguish Christian from non-Christian or orthodox from heretic—would certainly undermine the basis for so much of the disunity in the church and its separation into a plurality of denominations and confessions. Recognizing these differences as having to do with matters of opinion about academic questions that do not pertain to the essence of Christian faith and life would mean no longer focusing on them in such a way as to provoke disunity and separation. The proposal is consequently to this extent salutary.

To be a Christian is thus not to believe this or that speculative and controverted doctrine. Christian faith is no more a matter of speculative metaphysics and submission to ecclesial hierarchies than it is a matter of obedience to the commandments of the Law of Moses. Submission to the dogmas of the church is not among the positive demands of Jesus. Jesus only demands submission to his own teachings, which open up the kingdom of heaven to people here and now, which make it possible for people to live this human life in harmony with God, themselves, and others here and now, and his teachings mostly concern the form one's life takes, irrespective of the material conditions in which one finds oneself. Put another way: with the exception of baptism and the commemoration of his death in the Eucharist, Jesus does not demand that a person do anything in particular. He only demands that a person live his or her life, whatever it might be that he or she does with it, consistently with total love for God and for neighbor, as is fitting for someone whose Father is God himself. As Harnack puts the point:

> Positively what the Gospel says is this: Whoever you may be, and whatever your position, whether bondman or free, whether fighting or at rest—your real task in life is always the same. There is only one relation and one idea which you must not violate, and in the face of which all others are only transient wrappings and vain show: to be a child of God and a citizen of His kingdom, and to exercise love.[69]

This is what Jesus demands: a certain form of life that can be instantiated in any number of different contexts. And to be a Christian is thus to want to learn from Jesus alone and to be like him. It is to want to live the kind of life that he lived and that he taught others to live in one's own case, to be a part of this school and army whose mission is to live the life of the kingdom of heaven in this world. This was also Zwingli's opinion: "The

69. Harnack, *What is Christianity?*, 115–16.

whole of Christian life and salvation consists in this, that in Jesus Christ God has provided us with the remission of sins and everything else, and that we are to show forth and imitate Jesus Christ in our lives."[70] And Harnack once more: "No! the Christian religion is something simple and sublime; it means one thing and one thing only: eternal life in the midst of time, by the strength and under the eyes of God."[71] "Eternal life" means the lived experience here and now of the life of the kingdom of heaven.[72] It is "righteousness and peace and joy in the Holy Spirit" (Rom 14:17). It means enjoying one's life as someone reconciled to God. Once more, then, Christian faith is not first and foremost a matter of belief in a certain doctrine but rather a commitment and orientation of the heart toward Jesus whose teachings make this sort of life possible.

But then what should be done about these differences of theological opinion that do exist among Christians? Pannenberg correctly insists that a consensus arrived at by means of coercion is useless for determining the truth.[73] Christians should not seek unity by means of enforcing a particular answer to some disputed theological question. They might rather try to find ways to reconcile convergent opinions and to find a basis for them in Jesus's own teachings. Most of all, however, they should be willing to distinguish between the human word and the divine word. They must recognize when a human word does not have an adequate basis in the divine words of Jesus himself and so treat these human words as they deserve: as opinions and curiosities that may be true or false. Zwingli thus writes that "all those that teach in God's name should not sell their commands, ordinances, and burdens as God's, so that the yoke of his mercy should not become unpleasant to any one, but should leave them free."[74] One may be convinced of these opinions and find them quite helpful, but they cannot be forced upon people in the church if they cannot be shown to be the teachings of Jesus himself. Every person must know his or her place, and these debatable opinions certainly should not be confused with the actual clear teachings of Jesus as the principle of unity of any particular gathering.

Does this mean that nothing at all is beyond the pale in matters of religion? Does it mean that there is no such thing as damnable heresy any longer? No. But an opinion debated between two people does not become "beyond the pale" simply because a third party intervenes against it and

70. Zwingli, "Of Baptism," 145.

71. Harnack, *What is Christianity?*, 8.

72. Ladd, *Theology of the New Testament*, 293–95.

73. Pannenberg, *Systematic Theology*, 11.

74. Zwingli, "Liberty Respecting Food in Lent," 91.

threatens with excommunication anyone who disagrees. This would certainly be a show of pretended power, but it is not thereby also an unveiling of the truth. The truth or falsity of the opinion is not a matter of the risk of exclusion or death involved in believing it, as the example of Jesus himself shows.[75] Truth is a matter of speaking and thinking about a thing as it is; only the thing itself gives the truth. Introducing further disputants in a debate does not by itself resolve an issue, since only the thing itself being debated can resolve it. And the church does not debate about itself but about what Jesus teaches. This means that for Christians only the teachings of Jesus themselves can unconditionally dictate what is and is not appropriate in religion. The attitude of Zwingli is admirable in this respect: "I am deaf to such words as, 'It is heretical, erroneous, an offense to pious ears.'"[76] Such are the words of someone whose sole authority in theology is truth.

Everything demanded by Jesus is necessary, everything forbidden is out of bounds, and everything neither demanded nor forbidden is a matter of freedom. It may just be that the things thought necessary or forbidden by previous generations of Christians are not actually so; more things in the domain of theological opinion are matters of freedom than Christians have thought till now. There certainly is a damnable heresy: knowingly to reject Jesus. John taught very clearly: "No one who denies the Son has the Father" (1 John 2:23). One cannot get to God behind the back of Jesus. One cannot reject Jesus without also rejecting God, and everyone who refuses to sit at Jesus's feet and to be taught by him cannot be in a safe state. But it is one thing to accept Jesus and to wish to be his student, and it is another thing altogether to understand him in some particular way. Previous generations in the church were convinced that being an honest student of Jesus also means believing particular things in certain controversial questions, but Jesus himself did not teach this, and the present generation of Christians is no more beholden to all the convictions of those in the church who came before them in time than Jesus was to the "traditions of the elders."

---

75. See the discussion of Jesus as the "rebellious elder" in Bowker, *Jesus and the Pharisees*, 46–51.

76. Zwingli, *Commentary on True and False Religion*, 218.

7

Concluding Remarks

RECAPITULATION OF THE ARGUMENT

THIS BOOK HAS TRIED to argue for a "low" conception of ecclesial authority in theology. Its thesis has been that in the church God and Jesus alone exercise theological authority in an original, infallible, and in principle irreversible way. They alone always legitimately and successfully propose that something (not) be done for the sake of friendship with God. Every other person's exercise of theological authority is at best derivative. This means that no one has any other theological authority in the church except that of fallibly and in principle reversibly relating and bearing witness to the teachings of Jesus and to what God has done in him. These teachings and works are the only "tools" by which theological authority is exercised in the church.

This was proposed in opposition to the "high" conception of ecclesial authority in theology that was historically quite prominent in the church. This latter conception was analyzed in terms of the ideas called "traditionalism" and "hierarchy" above. "Traditionalism" refers to the idea that some group can make a binding and definitive decision about some matter of practice or belief on pain of exclusion from the group. This means that future would-be members of this group are beholden to the opinions and judgments of previous generations. It imposes a retrospective and "traditionalist" notion of group identity. "Hierarchy" refers to the idea that certain persons within a group occupy a rank which enables them to stipulate practices or behaviors to others in the group without the possibility of being questioned or contested. It means that not everyone within a group is equally authoritative within that group.

"Traditionalism" and "hierarchy" are closely related ideas. The "traditionalist" presumption to define the practice or belief of a group on pain of exclusion in such a way as to demand the submission of future generations can be buttressed by the appeal to the rank possessed by the persons making these definitions within the "hierarchy" of the group. The one idea thus supports and strengthens the other. These notions certainly played an integral role in the self-understanding of the religion of the Pharisees in Jesus's time, and they are likewise important to Roman Catholic theology in the present day. The Pharisees thought that God had granted to the rabbis the privilege of exercising "finality" within Judaism. This is to say that they could "bind" and "loose" in such a way as to interpret the Law bindingly and definitively for all subsequent generations. The Roman Catholic opinion understands God to guarantee the infallibility of the magisterium of the church in certain circumstances. He exercises a kind of "dual agency" together with this magisterium so that one could say at certain times that both the church and God himself are speaking. But Jesus does not agree with either of these ideas, and his teachings especially as related in the Gospel according to Matthew show this.

He rejects "traditionalism" as follows. On the one hand, he does not practice ritual handwashing even though it is a "tradition of the elders." On the other hand, he condemns the Pharisees for preferring the traditions of human beings to the commandments of God (Matt 15:1–9). In this way he distinguishes between the human word and the divine word. Only God's commandment can be unconditionally binding. Even authorized and officially sanctioned human traditions need not be obeyed, and they need positively to be disobeyed if they are contrary to the teaching of God. This implies that for Jesus every human word must always be measured against the standard of God's word. But this is only possible if the human word is always separable and distinct from God's word; the human word must always be one thing while the divine word is another. This means further that the work of human beings in exercising theological authority is testifying and bearing witness to God's teachings. They may succeed or fail in doing so, but no human word simply as such is granted "finality." God's word alone is final. This separability of divine and human word also means that God does not speak "through" human traditions. There is no "dual agency" by which the human word and the divine word would blend into each other. Only if the two are always separable and distinct can Jesus maintain that the human word must always be subordinated to the divine word. All this means that Jesus rejects "traditionalism."

He also condemns "hierarchy." Jesus maintains very clearly that all of his disciples are to think of each other as brothers and fellow students within his classroom (23:8–10). There is no differentiation of rank or privilege among them. Even the famous passage at Matt 16:17–19 poses no counterexample to this. There Simon receives the name "Peter" (*Petros*) because he recognizes Jesus as the Messiah and Son of God. His name is thus adjectival: he is "of (the) *petra*," which means that he recognizes Jesus as the rock (*petra*) on which the church will be built (16:18). Jesus then promises that he will give to Simon "keys" by which he will open and shut the kingdom of heaven for people. These keys are Jesus's teachings, and they open or shut depending on whether they are accepted or rejected. Likewise, Jesus commissions his apostles after his resurrection to go into the world and to make disciples of all nations by propagating his teachings (28:18–20). But they are not authorized to teach from themselves or to impose their own opinions on others. It consequently follows that no disciple of Jesus possesses such authority over the others as to be able to issue orders or make proposals without the possibility of being questioned or contested. The apostles and all Christians whatsoever have no further authority except that of bearing witness to the teachings of Jesus and to the works of God in him; these are the only "tools" left behind in the church for exercising theological authority. This is therefore how Jesus rejects "hierarchy."

The practice of the apostles in the New Testament agrees with this thesis. For example, they allow the gentiles to enter into the church by baptism without obliging them first to become Jews because God himself had already accepted them in giving them the Holy Spirit. They thus reject the contrary proposal of the Pharisee Christians who in any case were propagating an idea that Jesus himself had never mentioned. The apostles allow themselves to be guided only by Jesus's teachings and the works of God in him. Paul likewise addresses the problem of factions and rivalries in the Corinthian church surrounding preferred teachers by equally subordinating all to Jesus himself. Jesus alone is the foundation of the church; all teachers are simply his servants and stewards of the mysteries of God. There is nothing special about them in themselves, nor are they in any meaningful sense the objects of Christian faith. And John provides a wonderful example of this attitude in his epistle. He makes very clear that he and the other apostles do not pretend to do anything except to bear witness to what they have seen, heard, and held in their hands regarding Jesus. Their only job is that of passing on the commandment of God for all people: that all believe in the name of his Son and that they love each other. And these are more worthwhile preoccupations than those with which the church has been concerned in history.

SIGNIFICANCE OF THE THESIS

Jesus's rejection of the "traditionalism" and "hierarchy" of the Pharisees also motivates a rejection of the Roman Catholic system insofar as it is founded upon the same ideas. As regards the matter of theological authority, it is a system of ideas with no basis in Jesus's actual thinking and teaching. What else can be said at this point? What is the importance of the thesis that has been argued here? A few things are worth mentioning by way of conclusion.

Someone might wonder: Wouldn't it nevertheless be better if there were in fact a strictly derivative but functionally original theological authority in the church? Wouldn't it better if there were some always-present source to which one could appeal in order to resolve theological disputes? This is how Brandon Dahm argues: "Catholicism provides a mechanism for the kind of unity the Church needs: at the very least, doctrinal unity regarding the essentials of faith and a canon of Scripture."[1] Perhaps this would indeed be better—specifically to persons who are concerned about that sort of thing. But judgments of "better" or "worse" are often more informed by one's temperament and idiosyncratic concerns than by genuinely objective considerations. The presence of a functionally original theological authority in every generation is the sort of thing that would seem "better" to the sort of person that insists that every controversy must be resolvable and that everyone within a group must necessarily believe the same thing. It perhaps would seem "better" to one who prefers not to live with others who are different in matters one considers important or who cannot help but speculate about unclear things. But it need not seem "better" to a different sort of person. Dahm is offering an example of Adolf von Harnack's "old and almost ineradicable tendency of mankind to rid itself of its freedom and responsibility in higher things and subject itself to a law."[2] And elsewhere Harnack speaks of persons "whose chief endeavour is to find some authority in matters of religion" and "who are eager to be rid of their own responsibility and want to be reassured" as "putting religion on the Catholic plane; they want 'something they can lean upon.'"[3]

This is not to say that unity of belief is not valuable or important, but it is once more worth mentioning that there are other possible ways to unity. One might suggest that unity around the teachings actually left behind by Jesus would be better than unity in matters he never addressed. And the refusal to admit any such strictly derivative yet functionally original authority

---

1. Dahm, "That Great Revolution of Mind," 95.
2. Harnack, *What is Christianity?*, 118–19.
3. Harnack, *What is Christianity?*, 296.

in the church means that Christians do not need to consider themselves bound to past generations' opinions if these should show themselves over time to have disastrous consequences or be erroneous. Yet it must also be emphasized that it strictly does not matter what would purportedly be "better." What matters is what has actually been given. The concrete actions of God or Jesus in history cannot be reasoned about *a priori*. It is necessary to start with what has actually been done, rather than what one would have expected. Practical considerations arising out of a particular set of concerns and the preoccupations of a certain type of person do not determine the nature of the church; Jesus does. Human beings and their preferences do not dictate reality; only God does. Jesus has not left any such authority in the church; he has not left a way of definitively resolving every question that might ever arise to the inquiring mind. But he has left his teachings which open up the kingdom of heaven to those who accept them. These are the "tools" that have been left behind for the exercise of theological authority. One can thus infer from this fact that these teachings are more important than the things that have been debated and discussed *ad nauseam* in the history of Christian theology. And one can suggest that Christians ought to find their unity in the things Jesus has actually and clearly left the church, rather than in things he hasn't.

The conviction of the present author is that the vision argued for in this brief essay is salutary for Christian faith. Christians have too long been preoccupied with differences of opinion about speculative matters on which Jesus did not clearly pronounce in his teachings. They have been obsessed with getting the right answer to questions (especially those of a speculative metaphysical nature) for which there simply is not enough evidence. The churches have divided amongst themselves on the basis of differences of opinion about things that should only ever have been treated as matters of opinion and academic curiosities. These questions are admittedly fascinating. There is a certain pleasure to be had in contemplating them, and the conclusions one might draw by reflecting on them can prove spiritually edifying or useful in some way. But there is also a trap here. Persons with firm convictions about uncertain things come to think of Christianity itself as consisting in these speculative opinions and arcane subject matters. They come to identify faith in Jesus with very particular and well-defined theological convictions, since this is the shape that their own faith takes, and some have even tried to force their particular opinions on others by threat of death, excommunication, and damnation.

Consider how violence has marred the experience and testimony of the church throughout the ages.[4] How many laymen, priests, and bishops were exiled, tortured, maimed, and killed for maintaining an opinion that would later be accepted by many or even most! How many honest persons of good faith were put to death in horrible ways for holding to the "wrong" opinions at the wrong times in the wrong places! And how many of the points for which persons in the past killed or were killed are nevertheless debatable and still debated without resolution to the present day! The list of names is equally long and diverse. Among the most famous cases of victims of theological violence one could name: Arius and Athanasius who both suffered exile; the Donatists who were persecuted; Maximus the Confessor whose right hand and tongue were mutilated; the Albigensians who were slaughtered; Jan Hus who was burned at the stake after being promised safe passage; the Anabaptists who were drowned in Zürich; William Tyndale who was strangled and burned at the sake; Thomas More who was beheaded; Nicholas Ridley, Hugh Latimer, and Thomas Cranmer but also Michael Servetus who were burned at the stake; and the Waldensians who were nearly annihilated. The overconfidence with which Christians have held to their preferred speculations throughout history has served to justify persecution and instances of what in the present day could only be condemned as murder. It also goes without saying that there is nothing in Jesus's words that justifies the use of violence in defense of one's theological opinions. This holds true as much with regard to the literal physical violence of past generations as also to the *odium theologicum* and bigotry that characterize the faith of some today. These are sins to be repented of, rather than justified *ad hoc* by the invention of infallible and irreversible theological authorities of which Jesus never made mention nor any apostle dreamed.

Once more, this is not to say that there is no truth in theology. There is certainly a right and a wrong answer to the various questions that theologians have debated over the years. The very opinions of the catholic tradition may even all be true. But Christians should be more modest in their presumption to know the truth, in the opinions to which they firmly commit themselves, and in the questions they seek to investigate. It is one thing to be right about something, and it is another thing altogether to have enough evidence as to take the truth of one's opinions for granted in one's dealings with others. Too many Christians have spoken and still speak with such confidence about their opinions and doctrinal commitments that one would never get the impression that they are actually subject to considerable counter-arguments and laden with numerous theoretical problems. To what

4. See Evans, *Brief History of Heresy*, ch. 7.

end? The keys of the kingdom of heaven are the teachings that Jesus has actually left the church. To visit the sick person and to pray for one's friends and enemies alike: these are what will open up the kingdom to people; these are what will make a person to live in conformity with God's will; these are what will make God present to others and bring earth into harmony with heaven. One could say that these are the orders that Christ the captain has left the church as his army.

Yet it is admittedly far more convenient and easier to demand that others submit to obscure and speculative points of theology than it is to turn the other cheek (Matt 5:39) or to plan a banquet for "the poor, the crippled, the lame, and the blind" (Luke 14:13). It is often easier to be preoccupied with the perverse pleasure of endless theological disputation and to satisfy one's conscience with one's own orthodoxy than actually to go about doing good to the sick and the poor as Jesus did (Acts 10:38). It is easier to debate the possible meaningfulness of petitionary prayer in the light of a doctrine of divine providence than it is actually to pray for something with true faith and without giving up (Luke 18:1–8). Of course, one might say that these are not mutually exclusive courses of action—and yet only one of each of these pairs of alternatives is what Jesus actually taught. Jesus did not leave a mechanism for answering every question, but he did leave instructions about how a person ought to occupy his or her time. The perspective argued here is that it is better to spend one's efforts in the things Jesus actually taught than in the speculative questions that have preoccupied theologians for thousands of years. One should be satisfied with what God has seen fit to give in Jesus.

It might also be important to note here that the argument of this work is not at all novel. It in many ways agrees with Tertullian's discussion in his *On the "Prescription" of Heretics*. There are a few elements of his treatment worth emphasizing.

For example, Tertullian says that the heretics "treat of Scripture" as a matter of course: "for whence could they speak concerning the things of the Faith save out of the literature of the Faith?" (14). But the apostolic churches distinguish themselves from the heretics by the fact that they limit themselves to Scripture: "For, indeed, what is there opposed to us in our Scriptures? What have we introduced of our own so that we must remedy by omission or addition or alteration anything contrary to it which we have found in the Scripture? What we are, that the Scriptures are from the very beginning" (38). He is therefore clear that the teaching of the church must be grounded in and limited to what is found in Scripture. This is similar to the argument above: that the words of Jesus should form the substance of the church's teaching rather than traditions.

Tertullian is likewise incredulous that anyone should attribute ignorance to the apostles: "But who in his senses can believe that those men were ignorant of anything, whom the Lord gave to be teachers, keeping them close to himself in companionship, in discipleship, in society; to whom he was accustomed to explain privately whatever was obscure, saying that it was granted to them to know hidden truths which the people were not permitted to understand?" (22). Jesus withheld nothing from his apostles. They received his whole teaching, and these same apostles "faithfully handed on to the nations the rule received from Christ" (6). He discerns their teaching by appealing to the teachings of the apostolic churches throughout the whole world. And yet his summary of these teachings in the "rule of faith" contains nothing of the theological controversies of his years (13). There is no mention of æons or of a different God than the Creator and so on. But neither is there any mention of devotions to Mary or of her immaculate conception and assumption into heaven or of icons or of a doctrine of the Real Presence or anything of the sort! The conclusion he wishes to emphasize thus follows naturally in both cases: no such teachings were received from Jesus.

Tertullian further writes: "For the Son of God alone was it reserved to continue without fault" (3). All other persons of whatever rank or stature, whether "a bishop, or a deacon, or a widow, or a virgin, or a doctor, or even a confessor," can fall into heresy. This reality of human fallibility therefore means that a person's opinions are not to be accepted merely because of the "office" or position he or she occupies: "Do we test the Creed by persons or persons by the Creed?" (3). And he even says quite plainly that Jesus alone possesses original, infallible, and irreversible theological authority:

> For us, however, it is not lawful to introduce anything on our own authority, nor to choose that which any one else has similarly introduced. We have the Apostles of the Lord as our authorities, who not even themselves chose to introduce anything on their own authority, but faithfully handed on to the nations the rule received from Christ (6).

One could hardly ask for a better statement of the very thesis of the present work! Tertullian is clear: no one in the church may submit anything on his or her own authority. Not even the apostles did this; they only passed on what they learned from Jesus. And Tertullian also insists that the curious and debate-hungry should consult with the wise. These will tell them that "it is better for thee in the end to be ignorant, thus avoiding thy knowing what thou oughtest not, since thou already knowest what thou oughtest to know" in the plain teachings of Jesus and the apostles (14). Better not to know than to speculate and possibly to fall into harmful error.

The present work is thus far from offering a novel perspective. Quite to the contrary: more or less every substantial point argued in the pages above was already proposed by Tertullian nearly two thousand years ago in response to the heretical controversies of his day. He appreciated that ideas were being debated which could not be easily supported on the basis of Jesus's teachings. His appeal was in essence that the debates be set to the side and that all parties involved stick as closely as possible to what is clear in those dominical teachings. He wanted the church to define itself with reference to what Jesus taught. The teachings of Jesus as passed down by the apostles in the church were for him the only "tools" for exercising legitimate theological authority. The same argument is being made here as well. Tertullian's context was of course that of a proliferation of heresies. Each such heresy was built upon the speculative and unprovable interpretation of Scripture or else on the problematization of the sources of theology by appeal to secret traditions. The present context, by way of contrast, is that of a multitude of interminable theological disagreements and the radical proliferation of Christian confessions and denominations after two thousand years of theology. But the appeal is largely the same: differences about speculative matters should be left as matters of opinion; the plain teachings of Jesus are what matter most. This is how Tertullian argued, and this is how the present work argues as well.

This is not to say that everything Tertullian argues in the *"Prescription" of Heretics* is equally compelling today. He appealed to the succession of teachers in the churches founded by the apostles such as they were in his day in order to show that the ideas of the Gnostics are not of apostolic origin. This is an empirical argument of limited historical applicability. A similar argument can no longer be proposed in the present day, since two thousand years have passed and there is no longer any reliable guarantee that the churches founded by the apostles have preserved that teaching in its purity. Neither is this to say that Tertullian would agree with every proposition argued above. He certainly does not share the present author's attitudes towards heretics. But these are relatively unimportant points. What is most noteworthy is the substantial similarity of response to a situation of persistent theological disagreement.

As further evidence that the argument of the present work is not novel, consider that John of Damascus mentions in his enumeration of all "heresies" the so-called "*gnosimachi*." He says that these persons

> are opposed to all Christian knowledge, asserting that those who search the sacred Scriptures for some higher knowledge are doing something useless, because God requires of the Christian

nothing more than good deeds. Consequently, it is better to take a more simple course and not to be curious after any doctrine arrived at by learned research.[5]

It appears debatable whether there ever was a single well-defined group united around this principle.[6] In any case, this position is not so far from what has been argued here—with the qualification that it is not rightly called a "gnosimachy." What is being proposed is not an actual hatred of knowledge but rather a polemic against the unjustified presumption of knowledge. What John calls "learned research" has here been named "speculative metaphysics," and what John calls "good deeds" are here referred to as the teachings and commands of Jesus. The preoccupation of the Christian ought indeed to be the actual teachings of Jesus, not the dogmatic speculative proposals which—so it seems—many worry might be altogether abandoned if it weren't for the threat of ecclesial condemnation or damnation. And these teachings of Jesus are indeed practical and spiritual in nature, as the *gnosimachi* appreciated. They are principally concerned with how a person relates actively to God and to others. It is better to pray for a person in need, or to visit the sick, or in general to try to heal what for many is the open wound of their human life in the world, than to insist on pain of excommunication and by appeal to an unjustified pretense to infallibility that a person submit to a speculative thesis that can never be proven and for which there is only such evidence as would be ridiculed in any other field of inquiry than theology. The former actions are far better and more clearly attested in Jesus's words than the latter. The church should be a society for doing good. The parable of the sheep and the goats, for example, says nothing about speculative theological opinions but only about good done to those in need (Matt 25:31–46). Once more, James said it well: "Religion that is pure and undefiled before God the Father is this: to care for orphans and widows in their distress and to keep oneself unstained by the world" (Jas 1:27).

The point is not to undermine the church and to allow heresy to run wild, but rather to prevent an unfounded and unjustifiable pretense to functionally divine authority from causing unnecessary divisions in the church and getting in the way of an honest and good-faith search after theological truth. Neither is the point to undermine the authority of the teachings of Jesus and of the apostles, but rather to distinguish Jesus and his apostles from their later students and interpreters so as better to understand the former on their own terms. The point is certainly not to give everyone permission to believe whatever they please, but rather to set up truth rather than authority

---

5. John of Damascus, "On Heresies," 149.

6. Neander, *General History of the Christian Religion and Church*, 706–7.

as the sole and ultimate criterion of theological inquiry. Neither is the point to undermine the importance of doctrines, but rather to recognize the more fundamental and unifying character of one's personal commitment as a student to Jesus in comparison to all contested doctrinal opinions. The point is not to undermine belief in God or in Jesus, but rather to prevent Christians from inappropriately confusing or blending Jesus with a portion of his church in their mind. And the ultimate goal is to allow Jesus to speak for himself with respect to what he expects from his people and what his people can expect from him, i.e., to allow Jesus alone to dictate what it means to be his student.

The perspective presented here may not be convincing to everyone. It may seem audacious, even grossly implausible. But it was argued at length from the words of Jesus himself, and the point can be made once more that repentance is also necessary in this matter. There is no denying that the attitudes and theses argued for in the preceding pages is inconsonant with those that have been taken for granted in Christian theology and in the church for a very long time. But there is no simple obligation to think in the same way as those who came before. Even Jesus himself felt no obligation to share the concern of the "elders" for ritual handwashing before meals.

Consider once more the way that the apostles determined the question of whether or not to accept the gentiles in the church as gentiles. They saw that the gentiles had received the Holy Spirit without first becoming Jews. They saw that God had himself accepted the gentiles and that this imposed upon them the lesson that they should accept the gentiles as well. Something similar can therefore be said in the present day, as well. Some five hundred years have passed since the Protestant Reformation, and there are clearly persons accepted by God in every church or ecclesial community one can imagine. In every church one will find a person to whom God has borne witness by granting him or her the Holy Spirit. This is how God proves that he is no respecter of persons (Acts 10:34). He gives his Spirit even to those persons who disagree radically in matters of theology and who belong to different ecclesial communions. (Does one dare even to suggest that in the history of the church Christians with the Holy Spirit have with firm conviction put to death other Christians with the Holy Spirit?) One might therefore think that God means to be teaching the church the same lesson; it is necessary once more for the church to be led into the whole truth by the Holy Spirit (John 16:13). These persons are all accepted by God despite the theological opinions distinguishing them and even despite the fact that they may not accept one another; they too have been "conscripted" by him into his army, so to speak. And what more can a person need once he or she has received the Spirit?

The church has gone down the wrong path in history in the matter of theological authority. This is the pessimistic conclusion that ineluctably follows from the thesis and argumentation of the present essay. This is not to say that the church has failed or disappeared at any point in time, since it has always taught people to commit to Jesus in faith and to submit to his teachings, so that there have always been Christians in the world. But it is also true that many in the church have focused on the wrong things. They have been preoccupied with questions that are not as important as they have believed them to be. This is not to say that any of their opinions are false. Nothing about the present essay demands rejecting the theological opinions of the mainstream theological tradition. It is only that the church has pursued the question of the truth in the wrong way. It has set up mere human beings in the place of God and Jesus where they do not belong.

God and Jesus alone exercise theological authority in an original, infallible, and in principle irreversible way. No other person can claim such authority for him- or herself. God and Jesus alone can unconditionally and unqualifiedly demand that a person do or believe this or that for the sake of friendship with God. All human teachers can be and must think of themselves as no more than fallible witnesses testifying to what Jesus has taught and to what God has done in him. Anyone who wants to speak authoritatively in matters of Christian theology must appeal to the words of God and Jesus and not merely to traditions of whatever prestige and prominence which might exist among his students. All such traditions are simply what others within the community have said. God speaks for himself; Jesus too speaks for himself. Christian faith and theology should be a matter of wanting to learn out of mouth of God and of Jesus (to echo the words of Zwingli) what one ought to think and do.[7] As the Swiss reformer says elsewhere: "True piety demands, therefore, that one should hang upon the lips of the Lord and not hear or accept the word of any but the bridegroom."[8] And it may be that progress will be made in the ongoing discussions and debates of Christian theology when the disagreeing parties and witnesses dialog with one another by setting aside the pretense that they or anyone else can be something more than what they are: persons making a fallible and in principle reversible attempt to relate and bear witness to what God and Jesus have taught. Theological discussion can become productive when it is unimpeded by needless dogmatic commitments. And theologians may even find that Jesus really has nothing to say about the matter that they are debating. The discussion in that case can ultimately be

---

7. Zwingli, *Commentary on True and False Religion*, 62: "We wish to learn out of his own mouth what God is."

8. Zwingli, *Commentary on True and False Religion*, 92.

left to the side as a matter of opinion among Christians. But they certainly must dialog out of the shared conviction that they are equally Christians and students of one and the same Master, even despite their differences of opinion. And they must allow the words of Jesus and the works of God themselves rather than traditional ideas and inherited preconceptions to dictate what they as Christians ought to think and say and spend their time doing.

Bibliography

The Documents of Vatican II. Vatican City: Vatican, 2014.

Akin, Jimmy. *The Fathers Know Best: Your Essential Guide to the Teachings of the Early Church*. El Cajon: Catholic Answers, 2010.

———. *Teaching with Authority: How to Cut Through Doctrinal Confusion and Understand what the Church Really Says*. El Cajon: Catholic Answers, 2018.

Ambrose of Milan. *Exposition of the Christian Faith*. Translated by H. de Romestin et al. In *Nicene and Post-Nicene Fathers of the Christian Church*, Second Series, edited by Philip Schaff and Henry Wace, 10:199–314. Buffalo: Christian Literature, 1896.

Aristotle. *Metaphysics*. Translated by C. D. C. Reeve. Indianapolis: Hackett, 2016.

Athanasius. *Contra Gentes and De Incarnatione*. Translated by Robert W. Thomson. Oxford: Clarendon, 1971.

Augustine. *The Retractations*. Translated by Mary Inez Bogan. Washington, DC: Catholic University of America Press, 1968.

———. *Sermons on the New Testament*. Translated by R. G. MacMullen. In *Nicene and Post-Nicene Fathers*, Second Series, edited by Philip Schaff, 6:236–545. Buffalo: Christian Literature, 1888.

Ayres, Lewis. *Nicaea and Its Legacy: An Approach to Fourth-Century Trinitarian Theology*. New York: Oxford University Press, 2004.

Barth, Karl. *Church Dogmatics*. Translated by G. T. Thomson et al. Edinburgh: T. & T. Clark, 1936–1977.

Bates, Matthew W. *Salvation by Allegiance Alone: Rethinking Faith, Works, and the Gospel of Jesus the King*. Grand Rapids: Baker Academic, 2017.

Beaumont, Douglas M., ed. *Evangelical Exodus: Evangelical Seminarians and their Paths to Rome*. San Francisco: Ignatius, 2016.

Berger, Michael S. *Rabbinic Authority*. New York: Oxford University Press, 1998.

Bernier, Jonathan. *Rethinking the Dates of the New Testament: The Evidence for Early Composition*. Grand Rapids: Baker Academic, 2022.

Besong, Brian, and Jonathan Fuqua, eds. *Faith and Reason: Philosophers Explain Their Turn to Catholicism*. San Francisco: Ignatius, 2019.

Blomberg, Craig L. *Matthew*. Nashville: Broadman, 1992.

Bowker, John. *Jesus and the Pharisees*. New York: Cambridge University Press, 1973.

Bromiley, Geoffrey W., ed. *Zwingli and Bullinger*. Louisville: Westminster John Knox, 2007.

Brown, Raymond A. *The Epistles of John*. New York: Doubleday, 1982.

Budziszewski, J. "A Rake's Progress." In *Faith and Reason: Philosophers Explain Their Turn to Catholicism*, edited by Brian Besong and Jonathan Fuqua, 2–78. San Francisco: Ignatius, 2019.

Caragounis, Chrys C. *Peter and the Rock*. New York: Walter de Gruyter, 1990.

Carson, D. A. "Matthew." In *The Expositor's Bible Commentary*, 8:3–602. Grand Rapids: Zondervan, 1984.

Cassian, John. *On the Incarnation of the Lord, Against Nestorius*. Translated by C. S. Gibson. In *Nicene and Post-Nicene Fathers of the Christian Church*, Second Series, edited by Philip Schaff and Henry Wace, 11:547–621. Buffalo: Christian Literature, 1894.

Chadwick, Henry. "Ego Berengarius." *The Journal of Theological Studies* 40 (1989) 414–45.

Chrysostom, John. *Homilies on the Gospel of St. Matthew*. Translated by George Prevost. In *Nicene and Post-Nicene Fathers of the Christian Church*, First Series, edited by Philip Schaff, 10:1–515. Buffalo: Christian Literature, 1888.

Cowart, Jeremiah. "Crawl, Walk, Run: My Progression toward Mother Church." In *Evangelical Exodus: Evangelical Seminarians and their Paths to Rome*, edited by Douglas M. Beaumont, 71–82. San Francisco: Ignatius, 2016.

Crisp, Oliver D. *Analyzing Doctrine: Toward a Systematic Theology*. Waco, TX: Baylor University Press, 2019.

Dahm, Brandon. "That Great Revolution of Mind." In *Evangelical Exodus: Evangelical Seminarians and Their Paths to Rome*, edited by Douglas M. Beaumont, 83–106. San Francisco: Ignatius, 2016.

Denzinger, Heinrich. *The Sources of Catholic Dogma*. Translated by Roy J. Deferrari. Fitzwilliam: Loreto, 1955.

Evans, Craig A. *Matthew*. New York: Cambridge University Press, 2012.

Evans, G. R. *A Brief History of Heresy*. Malden: Wiley-Blackwell, 2003.

Fairbairn, Donald. *Grace and Christology in the Early Church*. New York: Oxford University Press, 2003.

Fee, Gordon D. *The First Epistle to the Corinthians*. Grand Rapids: Eerdmans, 1987.

France, R. T. *The Gospel according to Matthew: An Introduction and Commentary*. Downers Grove: InterVarsity, 1998.

Garland, David E. *Reading Matthew: A Literary and Theological Commentary*. Macon, GA: Smyth & Helwys, 2001.

Gundry, Robert H. *Matthew: A Commentary on His Literary and Theological Art*. Grand Rapids: Eerdmans, 1982.

———. *Peter: False Disciple and Apostate according to St. Matthew*. 2nd ed. Eugene, OR: Wipf & Stock, 2015.

Hagner, Donald. *Matthew 14–28*. Dallas: Word, 1995.

Hahn, Scott, and Kimberly Hahn. *Rome Sweet Home: Our Journey to Catholicism*. San Francisco: Ignatius, 1993.

Hanson, R. P. C. *The Search for the Christian Doctrine of God: The Arian Controversy 318–381*. Edinburgh: T. & T. Clark, 1988.

Harnack, Adolf von. *Outlines of the History of Dogma*. Translated by Edwin Knox Mitchell. New York: Funk & Wagnalls, 1893.

———. *What is Christianity?* Translated by Thomas Bailey Saunders. New York: G. P. Putnam's Sons, 1901.

Hart, David Bentley. *Tradition and Apocalypse: An Essay on the Future of Christian Belief*. Grand Rapids: Baker Academic, 2022.

Henry, Michel. *Words of Christ.* Translated by Christina M. Gschwandtner. Grand Rapids: Eerdmans, 2012.

Heschmeyer, Joe. *Pope Peter: Defending the Church's Most Distinctive Doctrine in a Time of Crisis.* El Cajon: Catholic Answers, 2020.

Hoehner, Harold W. *Ephesians: An Exegetical Commentary.* Grand Rapids: Baker Academic, 2002.

Holmes, Michael W. *The Apostolic Fathers: Greek Texts and English Translations.* 3rd ed. Grand Rapids: Baker Academic, 2007.

Horn, Trent. *The Case for Catholicism: Answers to Classic and Contemporary Protestant Objections.* San Francisco: Ignatius, 2017.

Irenaeus. *Against Heresies.* Translated by Alexander Roberts and William Rambaut. In *Ante-Nicene Fathers*, edited by Alexander Roberts et al., 1:315–567. Buffalo: Christian Literature, 1885.

John of Damascus. "On Heresies." In *Writings*, Translated by Frederic H. Chase Jr., 111–63. Washington, DC: Catholic University of America Press, 1958.

Johnson, Luke Timothy. *The Acts of the Apostles.* Collegeville, MN: Liturgical, 1992.

Josephus. *The Complete Works.* Translated by William Whiston. Nashville: Thomas Nelson, 1998.

Judisch, Neal. "Of Towers and Tongues." In *Faith and Reason: Philosophers Explain Their Turn to Catholicism*, edited by Brian Besong and Jonathan Fuqua, 97–124. San Francisco: Ignatius, 2019.

Keener, Craig S. *1–2 Corinthians.* New York: Cambridge University Press, 2005.

———. *Galatians.* New York: Cambridge University Press, 2018.

Kesich, Veselin. "Peter's Primacy in the New Testament and the Early Tradition." In *The Primacy of Peter: Essays in Ecclesiology and the Early Church*, edited by John Meyendorff, 35–66. Crestwood, NY: St. Vladimir's Seminary Press, 1992.

Kreeft, Peter. "Why?" In *Faith and Reason: Philosophers Explain Their Turn to Catholicism*, edited by Brian Besong and Jonathan Fuqua, 125–50. San Francisco: Ignatius, 2019.

Kruger, Michael J. *Canon Revisited: Establishing the Origins and Authority of the New Testament Books.* Wheaton, IL: Crossway, 2013.

Kruse, Colin G. *The Letters of John.* Grand Rapids: Eerdmans, 2000.

Küng, Hans. *Infallible? An Unresolved Inquiry.* Translated by John Bowden. New York: Continuum, 1994.

Ladd, George. *A Theology of the New Testament.* Grand Rapids: Eerdmans, 1993.

Leftow, Brian. "Anti Social Trinitarianism." In *Philosophical and Theological Essays on the Trinity*, edited by Thomas H. McCall and Michael C. Rea, 52–88. New York: Oxford University Press, 2009.

Leo the Great. *Letters.* Translated by Edmund Hunt. Washington, DC: Catholic University of America Press, 1957.

Levering, Matthew. *Was the Reformation a Mistake? Why Catholic Doctrine is Not Unbiblical.* Grand Rapids: Zondervan, 2017.

Maccoby, Hyam. *Early Rabbinic Writings.* New York: Cambridge University Press, 1988.

Mansoor, Menahem. "Pharisees." In *Encyclopedia Judaica*, edited by Fred Skolnik and Michael Berenbaum, 16:30–32. New York: Thomson Gale, 2017.

Marjanen, Antti, and Petri Luomanen, eds. *A Companion to Second-Century Christian "Heretics."* Boston: Brill, 2008.

McCall, Thomas H. *Analytic Christology and the Theological Interpretation of the New Testament*. New York: Oxford University Press, 2021.

———. *Which Trinity? Whose Monotheism? Philosophical and Systematic Theologians on the Metaphysics of Trinitarian Theology*. Grand Rapids: Eerdmans, 2010.

McGowan, Andrew B. *Ancient Christian Worship: Early Church Practices in Social, Historical, and Theological Perspectives*. Grand Rapids: Baker Academic, 2014.

McGuckin, John Anthony. *The Orthodox Church: An Introduction to Its History, Doctrine, and Spiritual Culture*. Malden: Wiley-Blackwell, 2007.

McKnight, Scot. "From Wheaton to Rome: Why Evangelicals Become Roman Catholic." *Journal of the Evangelical Theological Society* 45 (2002) 451–72.

Merleau-Ponty, Maurice. *Phenomenology of Perception*. Translated by Donald A. Landes. New York: Routledge, 2014.

Mitch, Curtis, and Edward Sri. *The Gospel of Matthew*. Grand Rapids: Baker Academic, 2010.

Moltmann, Jürgen. *The Trinity and the Kingdom: The Doctrine of God*. Translated by Margaret Kohl. Minneapolis: Fortress, 1993.

Moo, Douglas. *Galatians*. Grand Rapids: Baker Academic, 2013.

Mullins, R. T. "Classical Theism, Christology, and the Two Sons Worry." In *Impeccability and Temptation: Understanding Christ's Divine and Human Will*, edited by Johannes Grössl and Klaus von Stosch, 164–82. New York: Routledge, 2021.

———. *The End of the Timeless God*. New York: Oxford University Press, 2016.

Neander, Augustus. *General History of the Christian Religion and Church*. Translated by Joseph Torrey. Boston: Crock & Brewster, 1848.

Nemes, Steven. "Against Infallibility." *Criswell Theological Review* 19 (2021) 27–50.

———. *Orthodoxy and Heresy*. New York: Cambridge University Press, 2022.

———. *Theology of the Manifest: Christianity without Metaphysics*. Minneapolis: Lexington/Fortress Academic, 2023.

O'Collins, Gerald. *Tradition: Understanding Christian Tradition*. New York: Oxford University Press, 2019.

Origen. *On First Principles*. 2 vols. Translated by John Behr. New York: Oxford University Press, 2017.

Ott, Ludwig. *Fundamentals of Catholic Dogma*. Translated by Patrick Lynch. Fort Collins: Roman Catholic, 1954.

Pannenberg, Wolfhart. *Systematic Theology, Volume 1*. Translated by Geoffrey W. Bromiley. Grand Rapids: Eerdmans, 1991.

Parsenios, George. *First, Second, and Third John*. Grand Rapids: Baker Academic, 2014.

Paul VI, Pope. *Dei Verbum*. https://www.vatican.va/archive/hist_councils/ii_vatican_council/documents/vat-ii_const_19651118_dei-verbum_en.html.

———. *Lumen Gentium*. https://www.vatican.va/archive/hist_councils/ii_vatican_council/documents/vat-ii_const_19641121_lumen-gentium_en.html.

Peckham, John C. *Canonical Theology: The Biblical Canon, Sola Scriptura, and Theological Method*. Grand Rapids: Eerdmans, 2016.

Plantinga, Richard J., et al. *An Introduction to Christian Theology*. New York: Cambridge University Press, 2010.

Pliny the Younger. *Complete Letters*. Translated by P. G. Walsh. New York: Oxford University Press, 2006.

Prestige, G. L. *Fathers and Heretics*. London: Society for Promoting Christian Knowledge, 1940.

Rahner, Karl. *The Trinity.* Translated by Joseph Donceel. New York: Continuum, 1970.

Ratzinger, Joseph, Cardinal. *Called to Communion: Understanding the Church Today.* Translated by Adrian Walker. San Francisco: Ignatius, 1996.

Ray, Stephen K. *Upon This Rock: St. Peter and the Primacy of Rome in Scripture and the Early Church.* San Francisco: Ignatius, 1999.

Saldarini, Anthony J. *Pharisees, Scribes and Sadducees in Palestinian Society.* Grand Rapids: Eerdmans, 2001.

Schaff, Philip. *Creeds of Christendom with a History and Critical Notes.* Volume II: The Greek and Latin Creeds, with Translations. N.d.: Harper & Brothers, 1877.

Singer, Isidore, ed. *The Jewish Encyclopedia, Volume 3.* New York: Funk & Wagnalls, 1903.

Skolnik, Fred, and Michael Berenbaum, eds. *Encyclopedia Judaica, Volume 16: Pes–Qu.* 2nd ed. New York: Thomson Gale, 2017.

Stemberger, Günter. "The Pharisees and the Rabbis: How Much Continuity?" In *The Pharisees,* edited by Joseph Sievers and Amy Jill-Levine, n.d. Grand Rapids: Eerdmans, 2021.

Stewart, Alistair C. *The Original Bishops: Office and Order in the First Christian Communities.* Grand Rapids: Baker Academic, 2014.

Sullivan, Francis A. *From Apostles to Bishops: The Development of the Episcopacy in the Early Church.* New York: Newman, 2001.

———. *Magisterium: Teaching Authority in the Catholic Church.* Eugene, OR: Wipf & Stock, 1983.

Talbert, Charles H. *Matthew.* Grand Rapids: Baker Academic, 2010.

Tertullian. *On the Testimony of the Soul and The "Prescription" of Heretics.* Translated by T. Herbert Bindley. London: SCPK, 1914.

Torrance, Thomas F. *Scottish Theology: From John Knox to John McLeod Campbell.* Edinburgh: T. & T. Clark, 1996.

Tuggy, Dale. "Metaphysics and the Logic of the Trinity." *Oxford Handbooks Online,* 2016.

Turner, David L. *Matthew.* Grand Rapids: Baker Academic, 2008.

Vincent of Lérins. *Commonitorium.* Translated by C. A. Heurtley. In *Nicene and Post-Nicene Fathers,* Second Series, edited by Philip Schaff and Henry Wace, 11:123–59. Buffalo: Christian Literature, 1894.

Weger, Karl-Heinz. "Tradition." In *Encyclopedia of Theology: The Concise Sacramentum Mundi,* edited by Karl Rahner, 1728–34. New York: Seabury, 1975.

Wenkel, David H. "When the Apostles Became Kings: Ruling and Judging the Twelve Tribes of Israel in the Book of Acts." *Biblical Theology Bulletin: Journal of Bible and Culture* 42 (2012) 119–28.

White, Thomas Joseph. *The Light of Christ: An Introduction to Catholicism.* Washington, DC: Catholic University of America Press, 2017.

Yarbrough, Robert W. *1–3 John.* Grand Rapids: Baker Academic, 2008.

Zwingli, Ulrich. *Commentary on True and False Religion.* Edited by Samuel Macauley Jackson and Clarence Nevin Heller. Eugene, OR: Wipf & Stock, 2015.

———. "Concerning Choice and Liberty Respecting Food." In *Early Writings,* edited by Samuel Macauley Jackson, 70–112. Eugene, OR: Wipf & Stock, 1999.

———. "The Exposition of the Sixty-Seven Articles." In *Huldrych Zwingli Writings, Volume 1: The Defense of the Reformed Faith,* translated by H. Wayne Pipkin. Eugene, OR: Pickwick, 1984.

———. "Of Baptism." In *Zwingli and Bullinger,* edited by G. W. Bromiley, 129–75. Louisville: Westminster John Knox, 1953.

Index